More Loose Change

14 Quilts from Nickels, Dimes, and Fat Quarters

CLAUDIA PLETT AND LE ANN WEAVER

MM

D1716611

Martingale®
& COMPANY

More Loose Change:
14 Quilts from Nickels, Dimes, and Fat Quarters
© 2010 by Claudia Plett and Le Ann Weaver

That Patchwork Place® is an imprint of
Martingale & Company®.

Martingale & Company
19021 120th Ave. NE, Suite 102
Bothell, WA 98011 USA
www.martingale-pub.com

Printed in China
15 14 13 12 11 10   8 7 6 5 4 3 2 1

**Library of Congress Cataloging-in-Publication
Data is available upon request.**

ISBN: 978-1-56477-994-6

Dedication

To all those unsung heroes
out there—we mean all the
local quilt shop owners, who
tirelessly feed us with delicious fabrics, tools, classes,
books, and patterns.

Mission Statement
· ·
Dedicated to providing quality products
and service to inspire creativity.
· ·

CREDITS

President & CEO: Tom Wierzbicki
Editor in Chief: Mary V. Green
Managing Editor: Tina Cook
Developmental Editor: Karen Costello Soltys
Technical Editor: Nancy Mahoney
Copy Editor: Marcy Heffernan
Design Director: Stan Green
Production Manager: Regina Girard
Illustrator: Robin Strobel
Cover & Text Designer: Adrienne Smitke
Photographer: Brent Kane

Acknowledgments

Our thanks to:

Everyone at Martingale & Company, for their encouragement and expertise.

The nice folks at Warm & Natural, for their contributions.

And to Elizabeth Johnson, Regina Mann, and Scott Weaver, for their last-minute help with bindings and labels.

Contents

Introduction

Ready to spend some more of your loose-change fabrics? Of course we're talking about your *nickels, dimes, and quarters*—5" squares, 10" squares, and fat quarters of fabrics.

We have some brand new projects for you that we know will be at the top of your to-do list, and, as usual, perfectly suited to your skill level. Remember that most projects can be adjusted to your comfort zone. You can choose whether or not to appliqué, or add a scalloped or pieced border, etc. Fabric and "coin" requirements are given for each section of your project, making it easy for you or your local quilt shop to adjust the amounts you need. And again, look for the dollar signs at the beginning of each project. Here's what to expect:

$ = Easy: Simple piecing with no triangles

$$ = Intermediate: Piecing with lots of triangles or fusible appliqué

$$$ = Experienced: Hand appliqué or borders that are mitered or scalloped

Be sure to watch for our famous Piggy Bank Tips! Most projects lend themselves to a special designer tip just for you. We hope you can learn a new tidbit or trick to share with your friends.

As you browse through the projects, imagine each one in a themed colorway or as a scrappy project. If a project doesn't appeal to you in a red-and-black-and-white colorway, you might consider a different color combination. A project may have a black background, but you may find white or blue appeals to you more. We know these projects can be as versatile and varied as the quiltmakers who make them.

We're so thankful to have made new friends all over the world since the release of our first book *Loose Change* (Martingale & Company, 2008). We hear every day that quilters are forming classes, taking part in Internet swaps, using up their scraps, or purchasing those delicious charm packs and Layer Cakes available now. It's thrilling to be a part of it all!

Thank you all for spending *More Loose Change* with us!

- Claudia & Le Ann

Useful Information

On the following pages, we'll tell you all about nickels, dimes, and quarters and how you can use these irresistible stacks and bundles of fabrics to make the fun projects in this book.

What are Nickels, Dimes, and Quarters?

Very simply, nickels are 5" squares, dimes are 10" squares, and quarters refer to either a fat quarter that is 18" x 21" (½ yard of fabric, cut along the fold), or a ¼-yard cut that is 9" x 42".

You can convert dimes into nickels, and quarters into dimes or nickels. Below is an easy list for your reference.

Currency Conversion
1 dime = 4 nickels
1 fat quarter = 12 nickels *or* 2 dimes + 4 nickels

Prewashing

Be aware that when you purchase precut nickel or dime charm squares, they usually are not prewashed. If you prewash them, they will *not* be usable as nickels or dimes. To use them as is, you must forego prewashing. As a result, you might run the risk of colors bleeding when the quilt is washed the first time. Consider using dye magnets or color catchers (available at your local market or quilt shop) in the washer the first time the quilt is washed, or simply throw in an old white sock or terrycloth washcloth to absorb any bleeding color. Dye fixatives, such as Retayne, are also available at your local quilt shop; adding this type of product to the washer helps prevent fabric bleeding.

Where Do Nickels and Dimes Come From?

If you're not already making quilts using your loose-change fabric pieces, you'll quickly find that there are many, many sources for nickels and dimes!

Your own fabric stash will be your best source. Most quilters have built up fabric stashes that possibly could never be all used. The best way to get control of your stash is by using up what you have stuffed in drawers, shoe boxes, plastic tubs, closets, even luggage. When you cut up some of your stash, think of it as *recycling*!

Local quilt shops. Most shops today are wise to quilters' needs. You'll find them willing to provide exactly what you want. Almost every quilt shop has fat quarters precut from their fabrics and available at all times. They also stock precut nickel charms and dime Layer Cakes. You'll also find them agreeable to cutting some for you. Just ask!

Shop online. There are thousands of Internet quilt shops just aching to get your business! All you have to do is conduct a search using your favorite online search engine for "quilting charm packs," and you'll be amazed how many sources there are. You'll find that if the Internet shops don't have what you're looking for, just a phone call or email from you will result in whatever combinations you wish.

Swap with your friends. It can be fun! Plan a party or get-together with your quilting friends, your stitch group, or guild members. Tell each of them to bring bags of nickels, dimes, or fat quarters to share and exchange. Our local guild has their members bring 50 to 60 nickels cut from the same fabric (you can get 56 nickels from one yard of fabric). By the end of the meeting, they've been swapped and bagged, and each member takes home 50 to 60 different nickel charms.

Swap online. There are hundreds of online groups dedicated to swapping fabrics and blocks with online friends. You'll be surprised at how many specialize in nickel and dime swaps. You could enroll in a swap for different fabrics, such as creamy background prints, reproduction prints, juvenile prints, batiks, homespuns, or a swap based on color themes. It can be fun, and it's a great way to make friends with quilters from all over the world.

Old clothing. Some quilters horde old items of clothing for sentimental reasons. This is another source for small scraps that will easily convert into nickels and dimes. Some of the projects in this book are very suitable for shirtings, collected feed sacks, or any memory fabrics waiting for just the right artistic avenue.

Let's Talk a Little about Color

We all know that beauty is in the eye of the beholder. So when it comes to scrappy nickel or dime quilts, we feel the best colors to use are those you feel comfortable with. You may like working with bright neon colors, or you may enjoy muted or pastel fabrics.

What colors look best next to each other? We don't require the use of a color wheel. There! We said it! The projects in this book are mostly themed in a suggested color combination. However, we want to encourage you to try your own color themes. *More Loose Change* quilts are so versatile that we know your imagination will flourish with our designs. If, for example, you wish to make "Golden Goose" (page 36) in homespun plaids and a scrappy cream background instead of golds and yellows, we want to encourage you to do that.

There are no ugly fabrics. What you consider an ugly nickel may work very well as a small piece. Sometimes it will add a little sparkle to your work. Audition your pieces on your design wall and determine if they can be useful for you.

You might even find a place for that certain fabric on the back of your quilt. Pieced backs are wonderful to work with. You can swap with friends, and piece your entire backing from dimes or fat quarters, making use of those "unwanted" fabrics.

The chaos theory. Chaos can be a good thing! Be brave! Try new color combinations—the more the merrier. For example, you might not ever consider putting a brown piece next to a black, but if the value is right, it might just work. Although, if some of your blocks or pieces look too organized, you'll draw attention to that one area, and it will look like an error. This is one place where your design wall is your best friend. (See "Tools of the Trade," Design wall, on page 70.)

Detail of "Pumpernickel." In this quilt the chaos theory works when the value is right. (See the full quilt on page 53.)

. . . .

Adjacent colors. Try to keep like fabrics or like colors from touching each other in the quilt. Sometimes this can be unavoidable, but at least attempt it. If you have two like triangles meeting at an intersection, it may distort your design, or cause it to be lost altogether. Audition blocks on your design wall first; you may be able to solve the problem by simply rotating the block.

Detail of "Liquid Assets." Keep like fabrics from touching each other whenever possible. (See the full quilt on page 40.)

Value is the most important part of fabric selections. Value defines your quilt and can make or break your design. Value in nickels, dimes, or any scrap quilt basically comes down to light and dark. A golden yellow, for example, is light compared to a navy blue. But that same golden yellow is dark compared to an ivory. You might find yourself using lavender as a dark instead of a light. It doesn't matter, as long as the value remains consistent with the project instructions.

For example, in "Golden Goose" (page 36), there are countless different fabrics involved, but only two values—light and dark. The alternating value and contrast gives the quilt movement, interest, and beauty. Value within a fabric can be important also. If you have a wonderful blue calico, but it has some white flowers in it, you might find that fabric to be unsuitable, because, when placed next to other darks, all you will see is the little white flowers. It cannot be classified as either light or dark.

In most cases, however, the main value of printed fabrics is found in the background of that print. If your fabric has a deep red background with green vines on it, it will most likely read as dark. If those same green vines were on a pink background, it would most likely read as a light.

If you're having trouble determining the value of several pieces together, use a photocopier to make a black-and-white copy. You can use this technique to eliminate any troublemakers in the group.

Value can be important when positioning blocks into rows. Just as you would not want to have two like colors adjacent to each other, the same holds true with values. For example, where two blocks intersect, you don't want two or three light-value fabrics touching each other. Otherwise, when the quilt is assembled, your eye will be drawn to those groups of light values, and it will be distracting. The same holds true with dark fabrics touching each other.

Some quilters use their digital cameras as a design placement tool. You can arrange blocks on the wall and take a picture. After several arrangements you can refer to the pictures to see which arrangement works best. Once again, your design wall becomes your best friend. Use it!

Detail of "Crown Jewels." Light and dark values create a vibrant design. (See the full quilt on page 15.)

About More Loose Change

Look for the $ symbol at the beginning of each project. Remember that some projects may be simplified or adjusted to suit your skill level. Whether or not to use appliqué in a project is up to you and your comfort zone.

Some projects may be suitable for multiple nickels or dimes of the same fabrics. Other projects seem more suited to a wider variety of fabrics to obtain the ultimate scrappy appearance. Simply put, the more fabrics you use, the more scrappy your quilt will appear. Keep this in mind if you're making one of the small projects; you might prefer to use only nickels or dimes, and not fat quarters.

Also, some projects call for half-square-triangle units. Our instructions always have you make them just a bit larger than required so that you can then trim them down to the proper measurement. This makes cutting easier since there are no ⅞" measurements and ensures the accuracy of your triangle units.

Now on to the projects. Let's begin!

Bright Bullion

Designed, pieced, and machine quilted by Le Ann Weaver

Finished quilt: 70½" x 92½"
Finished block: 8" x 20"
SKILL LEVEL: $

Nothing could be faster or easier than making this quilt! Use a dozen fat quarters and a little yardage in any color you choose, and make this quilt for a gift, a charity quilt, or even to keep for yourself.

Materials

FAT QUARTERS

12 assorted prints for blocks*

If, after prewashing and trimming off the selvage, the fat quarters do not measure at least 18" x 21", you'll need 15 fat quarters.

ADDITIONAL FABRIC AND SUPPLIES

2 yards of green print for sashing and inner border
1¼ yards of fabric for outer border
⅔ yard of blue fabric for binding
6 yards of fabric for backing
75" x 97" piece of batting

Cutting

From the *18" width* of *each* fat quarter, cut:
6 strips, 3½" x 18" (72 total)

From the green print, cut:
24 strips, 2½" x 42"
8 rectangles, 1¾" x 2"
8 rectangles, 1¾" x 4½"

From the outer-border fabric, cut:
8 strips, 4½" x 42"
4 squares, 2" x 2"

From the blue binding fabric, cut:
9 strips, 2¼" x 42"

Making the Blocks

1. Randomly sew six of the fat quarter 3½"-wide strips together as shown to make a strip set. Make 12 strip sets. Press the seam allowances in one direction. Cut each strip set into two 8½"-wide units, 24 total.

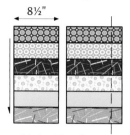

Make 12 strip sets.
Cut 24 units.

Piggy Bank Tip

Perfect Ruler
An 8½" x 24" ruler is perfect for this project!

2. Using six green 2½"-wide strips, sew four units to each strip as shown. Cut apart the blocks, trimming the green strips even with the edges of the units. Press the seam allowances toward the green strip. The blocks should measure 8½" x 20½". Make 24 blocks.

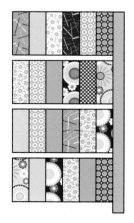

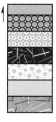

Make 24.

Bright Bullion

9

Assembling the Quilt Top

1. Sew four blocks together end to end as shown to make a block row. Make six rows. Each block row should measure 8½" x 80½".

Make 6.

2. Sew 10 of the green 2½"-wide strips together in pairs, end to end, and then trim each strip to measure 80½" long. Make five sashing strips.

3. Join the block rows and the five sashing strips as shown with the sashing strips between the block rows, rotating every other row 180° as shown. The quilt center should measure 58½" x 80½".

Adding the Borders

1. For the inner border, sew the remaining green 2½"-wide strips together end to end. Refer to "Adding Borders" on page 73 to cut two strips the length of the quilt for the side borders. Add the side borders, pressing the seam allowances toward the borders. Measure the width of the quilt and cut two strips for the top and bottom borders. Add the top and bottom borders and press. The quilt center should measure 62½" x 84½".

2. To make the corner blocks for the outer border, sew green 1¾" x 2" rectangles to opposite sides of an outer-border fabric 2" square. Then sew green 1¾" x 4½" rectangles to the top and bottom of the block as shown. Make four corner blocks.

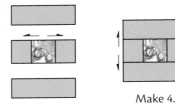

Make 4.

3. Sew the 4½"-wide outer-border strips together end to end. Measure your quilt through the center in both directions and cut two side borders and two top and bottom borders to the correct measurements.

4. Stitch the side borders to your quilt top. Press the seam allowances toward the inner border.

5. Stitch the corner blocks to the ends of the top and bottom borders, and then sew the borders to your quilt top. Press the seam allowances toward the inner border.

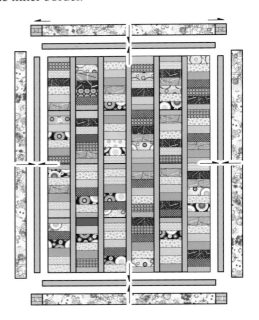

Finishing Your Quilt

1. Assemble the quilt sandwich and quilt as desired.

2. Using the blue 2¼"-wide binding strips, make and attach double-fold binding.

Christmas Bonus

Designed and pieced by Claudia Plett; machine quilted by Le Ann Weaver

Finished quilt: 72½" x 88½"
Finished block: 8" x 8"
SKILL LEVEL: $$

A beautiful yet easy quilt to create for the holidays—or any other time of the year! We used pale pink prints as our background, but we can envision the same design using perhaps a light blue or basic cream background. Just add three colors and voilà!

Materials

DIMES

37 pale pink background prints for blocks (or 148 nickels, or 13 fat quarters)

19 pale pink background prints for border (or 76 nickels, or 7 fat quarters)

15 red prints for blocks (or 60 nickels, or 5 fat quarters)

18 green prints for blocks (or 72 nickels, or 6 fat quarters)

10 blue prints for blocks (or 40 nickels, or 4 fat quarters)

ADDITIONAL FABRIC AND SUPPLIES

5¾ yards of fabric for backing

1 yard of red print for bias binding (or ⅔ yard for straight-grain binding)

77" x 93" piece of batting

Cutting

From *each* dime for blocks, cut:
4 squares, 5" x 5" (320 total)

From the 19 dimes for borders, cut a *total* of:
1 square, 5" x 5"
75 squares, 4½" x 4½" (1 is extra)

From the red print for binding, cut:
1½" bias strips to total 350" for single-fold bias binding *OR* 9 strips, 2¼" x 42", for double-fold straight-grain binding

Making the Blocks

1. Refer to "Creating Half-Square-Triangle Units" (page 71) and use 48 red squares and 48 pink squares to make 96 of half-square-triangle unit A as shown. Press the seam allowances toward the red triangles.
2. Use 60 green squares and 60 pink squares to make 120 of half-square-triangle unit B as shown. Press the seam allowances toward the green triangles.
3. Use 40 blue squares and 40 pink squares to make 80 of half-square-triangle unit C as shown. Press the seam allowances toward the blue triangles.
4. Use 12 red squares and 12 green squares to make 24 of half-square-triangle unit D as shown. Press the seam allowances toward the green triangles.

Unit A.
Make 96.

Unit B.
Make 120.

Unit C.
Make 80.

Unit D.
Make 24.

5. Trim all of the half-square-triangle units to measure 4½" x 4½".

6. Sew three A units and one C unit together as shown to make block E. Press as indicated, referring to "Pressing" (page 70). Make a total of 32 of block E.
7. Sew three B units and one C unit together as shown to make block F and press. Make a total of 24 of block F.
8. Sew two B units, one C unit, and one D unit together as shown to make block G; press. Make a total of 24 of block G. All of the blocks should measure 8½" x 8½".

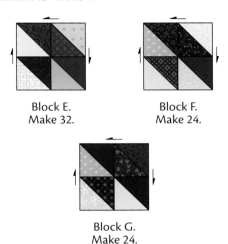

Block E.
Make 32.

Block F.
Make 24.

Block G.
Make 24.

Assembling the Quilt Top

1. Lay out the blocks in 10 rows of eight blocks each, referring to the diagram for block placement and rotating the blocks as shown. Sew the blocks together in rows and press the seam allowances in opposite directions from row to row.
2. Sew the rows together, pressing the seam allowances in one direction to complete the quilt center.

Adding the Border

We used a notched border for our quilt. If you choose to use a straight-edged border instead, trim the pink 5" square to 4½" and use a total of 76 pink 4½" squares. If you choose to use our notched border, follow these steps:

1. Measuring 1" from the corner of a pink 4½" square and using a ruler marked with a 45° line, trim away the corner at a 45° angle as shown. Trim 22 of the 4½" pink squares.

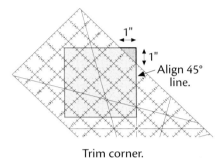

1"

1"

Align 45° line.

Trim corner.

2. Sew the notched squares in pairs as shown.

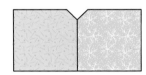

3. Cut the 5" pink square in half diagonally to make two half-square triangles for the corners on the bottom border. (The top border doesn't have notches.)
4. For the side borders, sew 12 pink 4½" squares and four notched pairs together as shown to make a border strip. Make two and sew them to the sides of your quilt top. (If you're making a straight-edged border, sew 20 squares together for each side border.)

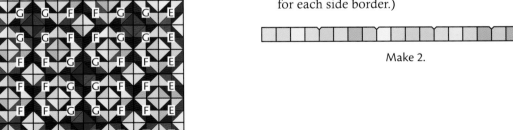

Make 2.

5. For the bottom border, sew 10 pink 4½" squares and three notched pairs together to make a border strip. Add a corner triangle to each end as shown. Sew the border to the bottom of your quilt. (If you're making a straight-edged border sew 18 squares together for the bottom border.)

Make 1.

6. For the top border, sew 18 pink 4½" squares together to make a border strip. Sew the border to the top of your quilt.

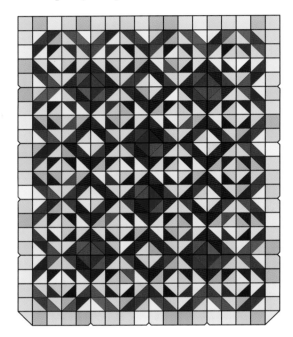

Finishing Your Quilt

1. Assemble the quilt sandwich and quilt as desired.
2. Using the red print strips, make and attach single-fold bias binding. (For a straight-edged quilt, make and attach double-fold binding.)

Crown Jewels

Designed, pieced, and machine quilted by Le Ann Weaver

Finished quilt: 81½" x 81½"
Finished block: 13½" x 13½"
SKILL LEVEL: $$

Talk about brilliance! This quilt is a very flashy way to show off your piecing skills with silvers, golds, rubies, jades, and amethysts—a precious treasure sure to please.

Materials

FABRIC	YOUR CHOICE OF:	
	DIMES	FAT QUARTERS
Assorted amethyst prints for blocks and outer border	35	13
Assorted gold prints for blocks and outer border	31	9
Assorted jade prints for blocks and outer border	24	8
Assorted ruby prints for blocks and outer border	51	15
Assorted silver prints for blocks and outer border	66	20

Additional Fabric and Supplies

¾ yard of silver print for inner border
7½ yards of fabric for backing
⅔ yard of ruby print for binding
86" x 86" piece of batting

Cutting

FABRIC	YOUR CHOICE OF:	
	DIMES	**FAT QUARTERS**
Assorted amethyst prints	**From *each of 11* dimes, cut:** 9 squares, 2¾" x 2¾" (99 total, 3 are extra) **From *each of 24* dimes, cut:** 4 squares, 5" x 5" (96 total, 3 are extra)	**From *each of 10* fat quarters, cut:** 6 squares, 5" x 5" (60 total) 10 squares, 2¾" x 2¾" (100 total, 4 are extra) **From *each of 3* fat quarters, cut:** 11 squares, 5" x 5" (33 total)
Assorted gold prints	**From *each of 28* dimes, cut:** 9 squares, 2¾" x 2¾" (252 total, 4 are extra) **From *each of 3* dimes, cut:** 4 squares, 5" x 5" (12 total)	**From *each of 6* fat quarters, cut:** 36 squares, 2¾" x 2¾" (216 total) **From 1 fat quarter, cut:** 12 squares, 2¾" x 2¾" **From *each of 2* fat quarters, cut:** 6 squares, 5" x 5" (12 total) 10 squares, 2¾" x 2¾" (20 total)
Assorted jade prints	**From *each* of the 24 dimes, cut:** 6 rectangles, 2¾" x 5" (144 total, 4 are extra)	**From *each* of the 8 fat quarters:** 18 rectangles, 2¾" x 5" (144 total, 4 are extra)
Assorted ruby prints	**From *each of 32* dimes, cut:** 9 squares, 2¾" x 2¾" (288 total, 8 are extra) **From *each of 8* dimes, cut:** 6 rectangles, 2¾" x 5" (48 total) **From *each of 11* dimes, cut:** 9 squares, 2¾" x 2¾" (99 total, 3 are extra)	**From *each of 8* fat quarters, cut:** 35 squares, 2¾" x 2¾" (280 total) **From *each of 3* fat quarters, cut:** 16 rectangles, 2¾" x 5" (48 total) **From *each of 4* fat quarters, cut:** 24 squares, 2¾" x 2¾" (96 total)
Assorted silver prints	**From *each of 12* dimes, cut:** 4 squares, 5" x 5" (48 total) **From *each of 17* dimes, cut:** 9 squares, 2¾" x 2¾" (153 total, 1 is extra) **From *each of 21* dimes, cut:** 9 squares, 2¾" x 2¾" (189 total, 5 are extra) **From *each of 16* dimes, cut:** 6 rectangles, 2¾" x 5" (96 total, 4 are extra)	**From *each of 4* fat quarters, cut:** 12 squares, 5" x 5" (48 total) **From *each of 5* fat quarters, cut:** 30 squares, 2¾" x 2¾" (150 total) **From *each of 5* fat quarters, cut:** 35 squares, 2¾" x 2¾" (175 total; 1 is extra) **From *each of 5* fat quarters, cut:** 18 rectangles, 2¾" x 5" (90 total) **From 1 fat quarter, cut:** 16 squares, 2¾" x 2¾" 2 rectangles, 2¾" x 5"

Additional Cutting

From the silver print for inner border, cut:
8 strips, 2¾" x 42"

From the ruby print for binding, cut:
9 strips, 2¼" x 42"

Making the Blocks

1. Referring to "Creating Quick Corner Units" (page 71) and using a light-colored pencil, mark a diagonal line on the wrong side of each amethyst, gold, silver, and ruby 2¾" square.

Piggy Bank Tip

Bonus "Quickies"

Make use of those triangles you would normally throw away when making quick-corner units. Draw a second line ½" from your diagonal line on the 2¾" squares. Sew on *both* lines, and then cut between the two stitching lines. Press the resulting triangles open. Save your quickies for another project!

2. Place gold 2¾" squares on diagonally opposite corners of 76 amethyst 5" squares as shown, right sides together. Stitch on the drawn line and trim away the corner fabric, leaving a ¼" seam allowance. Press the seam allowances toward the gold triangles. Sew silver 2¾" squares to the remaining two corners as shown. Press the seam allowances toward the silver triangles. Make 76 A units.

Unit A.
Make 76.

3. Repeat step 2 using 48 silver 5" squares, the remaining gold squares, and 96 ruby squares from step 1. Make 48 B units.

Unit B.
Make 48.

4. Use 92 jade rectangles and 184 silver 2¾" squares to make 92 flying-geese units as shown, using the quick-corner technique. Use the silver rectangles and 184 ruby squares to make 92 flying-geese units. Use the remaining jade rectangles and ruby squares to make 48 flying-geese units. Use the ruby rectangles and amethyst 2¾" squares to make 48 flying-geese units. Press the seam allowances toward the corners. (Set aside the four remaining silver squares for the outer-border corner blocks.)

Make 92.   Make 92.

Make 48.   Make 48.

5. Sew the flying-geese units together in pairs as shown. Make 92 C units and 48 D units.

Unit C.   Unit D.
Make 92.   Make 48.

6. Sew two A units and one C unit together, rotating the units as shown. Make 26 block units.

Make 26.

7. Sew C units to opposite sides of each amethyst 5" square as shown. Make 13 center units. (Set aside the four remaining amethyst squares for the outer-border corner blocks.)

Make 13.

8. Lay out two units from step 6 and one center unit from step 7 as shown. Sew the units together to make block E. Make 13 blocks.

Block E.
Make 13.

9. Repeat steps 6–8 using the B units, D units, and the gold 5" squares to make 12 F blocks.

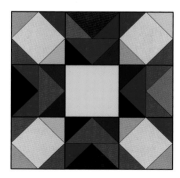

Block F.
Make 12.

Assembling the Quilt Top

1. Lay out the E and F blocks as shown. For row 1, sew three E blocks and two F blocks together. Make three of row 1. For row 2, sew three F blocks and two E blocks together. Make two of row 2. Press the seam allowances toward the F blocks.

Row 1.
Make 3.

Row 2.
Make 2.

2. Sew the rows together, alternating them as shown. Press the seam allowances in one direction.

Adding the Borders

1. For the inner border, sew the silver 2¾"-wide strips together end to end. Refer to "Adding Borders" (page 73) to cut two strips the length of the quilt for the sides. Add the side borders, pressing the seam allowances toward the borders. Measure the width of the quilt and cut two strips for the top and bottom borders. Add the top and bottom borders and press the seam allowances toward the borders. Your quilt center should measure 72½" x 72½".

2. Using the quick-corner method, sew one silver 2¾" square to one amethyst 5" square as shown. Press the seam allowances toward the silver triangle. Make four corner blocks.

Make 4.

3. Lay out six A units and 10 C units as shown. Sew the units together to make a border strip. Make four border strips.

A C C A C C A C C A C C A C C A

4. Sew two border strips to the sides of your quilt top. Press the seam allowances toward the inner border.

5. Sew corner units to the ends of the two remaining border strips as shown. Sew the border strips to the top and bottom of your quilt top. Press the seam allowances toward the inner border.

Finishing Your Quilt

1. Assemble the quilt sandwich and quilt as desired.

2. Using the ruby 2¼"-wide strips, make and attach double-fold binding.

Down the Drain

Designed and pieced by Claudia Plett; machine quilted by Le Ann Weaver

Finished quilt: 53" x 53"
Finished block: 7½" x 7½"
SKILL LEVEL: $$

The blocks create a lot of motion in this stunning quilt made with water-themed nickels. What a great kid's quilt or wall hanging!

Materials

NICKELS

112 assorted light blue prints for blocks and borders (or 28 dimes, or 10 fat quarters)
123 assorted dark blue prints for blocks and borders (or 31 dimes, or 11 fat quarters)

ADDITIONAL FABRIC AND SUPPLIES

3½ yards of fabric for backing
½ yard of light blue print for binding
57" x 57" piece of batting

Cutting

From *each of* 32 assorted light blue print nickels, cut:
4 squares, 2⅜" x 2⅜" (128 total)

From *each of* 43 assorted dark blue print nickels, cut:
4 squares, 2⅜" x 2⅜" (172 total)

From *each of* 26 assorted light blue print nickels, cut:
1 square, 2¾" x 2¾" (26 total)

From *each of* 26 assorted dark blue print nickels, cut:
1 square, 2¾" x 2¾" (26 total)

From *each of* 18 assorted light blue print nickels, cut:
1 square, 5" x 5"; cut into quarters diagonally to yield 72 A triangles

From *each of* 18 assorted dark blue print nickels, cut:
1 square, 5" x 5"; cut into quarters diagonally to yield 72 A triangles

From *each of* 36 assorted light blue print nickels, cut:
1 square, 4⅝" x 4⅝"; cut in half diagonally to yield 72 B triangles

From *each of* 36 assorted dark blue print nickels, cut:
1 square, 4⅝" x 4⅝"; cut in half diagonally to yield 72 B triangles

From the light blue binding fabric, cut:
6 strips, 2¼" x 42"

Making the Blocks

1. Using the light blue and dark blue 2⅜" squares, randomly sew two light blue squares and two dark blue squares together to make a four-patch unit as shown. Press as indicated, referring to "Pressing" (page 70). Make 36 units, each measuring 4¼" x 4¼".

Make 36.

2. Making sure to position all of the four-patch units as shown with the light blue squares on the upper right and lower left; sew two different light blue A triangles to opposite sides of the unit as shown. Press the seam allowances toward the triangles. Sew two different dark blue A triangles to the remaining sides as shown and press.

3. Again, making sure the light blue squares are positioned as shown, sew two different light blue B triangles to the unit from step 2. Press the

seam allowances toward the just-added triangles. Then, sew two different dark blue B triangles to the remaining sides to complete the block; press. Your blocks should each measure 8" x 8". Make 36 blocks.

Make 36.

Assembling the Quilt Top

1. For easy assembly, sew the blocks in units of four blocks each, rotating the blocks so that four dark blue B triangles meet in the center as shown. (See "Design Wall" tip below.) Press as indicated. Make nine units.

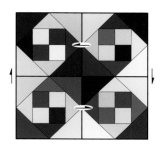

Make 9.

2. Sew the four-block units into three rows of three units each. Press the seam allowances in opposite directions from one row to the next. Then stitch the rows together.

Piggy Bank Tip

Design Wall

Try using a design wall (see "Tools of the Trade," Design wall on page 70) to position your blocks to keep identical fabrics from touching each other. Have fun rotating them—but don't get dizzy!

Adding Borders

1. For the side inner border, sew together 24 dark blue 2⅜" squares. Press the seam allowances in

one direction. Make two and sew them to the sides of your quilt center. Press the seam allowances toward the inner border.

2. Make two more inner borders using 26 dark blue 2⅜" squares for each border. Sew these borders the top and bottom of your quilt center. Press the seam allowances toward the inner border.

3. Referring to "Creating Half-Square-Triangle Units" (page 71), use the 26 dark blue and 26 light blue 2¾" squares to make 52 half-square-triangle units. Press the seam allowances toward the dark blue triangles. Your units should measure 2⅜" x 2⅜".

4. Sew 13 half-square-triangle units and 13 light blue 2⅜" squares together to make an outer-border unit. Press the seam allowances toward the light blue squares. Make four outer-border units.

Make 4.

5. Sew two borders to the sides of your quilt top. Press the seam allowances toward the inner border. Add a light blue 2⅜" square to each end of the two remaining border units, and then sew them to the top and bottom of your quilt as shown. Press the seam allowances toward the inner borders.

Finishing Your Quilt

1. Assemble the quilt sandwich and quilt as desired.
2. Using the light blue 2¼"-wide binding strips, make and attach double-fold binding.

Easy Money

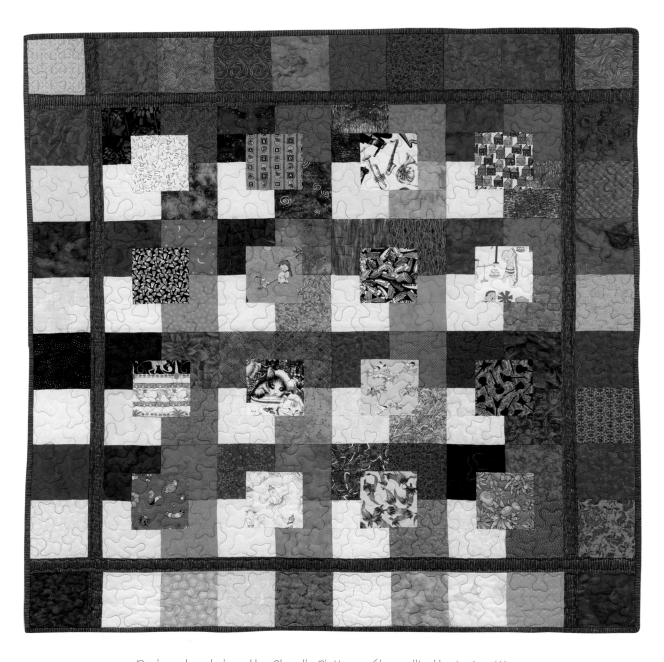

Designed and pieced by Claudia Plett; machine quilted by Le Ann Weaver

Finished quilt: 42½" x 42½"
Finished block: 8" x 8"
SKILL LEVEL: $

This is one of those quilts that seems just too easy to believe. It's a quick gift for any baby shower, wall hanging, or charity quilt. You'll have fun choosing just the right prints for the block centers!

Materials

NICKELS

16 assorted novelty prints for blocks (or 4 dimes, or 2 fat quarters)
25 assorted blue prints for blocks and border (or 7 dimes, or 2 fat quarters)
25 assorted red prints for blocks and border (or 7 dimes, or 2 fat quarters)
25 assorted yellow prints for blocks and border (or 7 dimes, or 2 fat quarters)
25 assorted green prints for blocks and border (or 7 dimes, or 2 fat quarters)

ADDITIONAL FABRIC AND SUPPLIES

⅔ yard of purple print for inner borders and binding
2⅞ yards of fabric for backing
47" x 47" piece of batting

Cutting

From each of the 16 assorted novelty print nickels, cut:
1 square, 4½" x 4½" (16 total)

From each of 16 assorted blue print nickels, cut:
1 rectangle, 2½" x 4½" (16 total)*
1 square, 2½" x 2½" (16 total)*

From each of 16 assorted red print nickels, cut:
1 rectangle, 2½" x 4½" (16 total)*
1 square, 2½" x 2½" (16 total)*

From each of 16 assorted yellow print nickels, cut:
1 rectangle, 2½" x 4½" (16 total)*
1 square, 2½" x 2½" (16 total)*

From each of 16 assorted green print nickels, cut:
1 rectangle, 2½" x 4½" (16 total)*
1 square, 2½" x 2½" (16 total)*
Keep like fabric pieces together in sets for the blocks.

From each of 9 assorted blue print nickels, cut:
1 square, 4½" x 4½" (9 total)

From each of 9 assorted red print nickels, cut:
1 square, 4½" x 4½" (9 total)

From each of 9 assorted yellow print nickels, cut:
1 square, 4½" x 4½" (9 total)

From each of 9 assorted green print nickels, cut:
1 square, 4½" x 4½" (9 total)

From the purple fabric, cut:
5 strips, 2¼" x 42"
6 strips, 1½" x 42"; crosscut 3 of the strips into:
   2 strips, 1½" x 32½"
   4 rectangles, 1½" x 4½"

Making the Blocks

For each block, you'll need one novelty print 4½" square and one set (one 2½" square and one 2½" x 4½" rectangle) of *each* color (blue, red, yellow, and green).

1. Sew a yellow square and a blue square together. Then sew a green square and a red square together. Press the seam allowances as indicated. Sew units to opposite sides of your novelty square, making sure to position the colors as shown. Press the seam allowances toward the novelty square.

       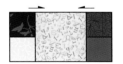

2. Sew a yellow rectangle and a green rectangle together end to end. Then sew a blue rectangle and a red rectangle together. Press the seam allowances as indicated. Sew the units to the partial block as shown. Your block should measure 8½" x 8½". Make a total of 16 blocks, making sure to maintain the same color positions in each block.

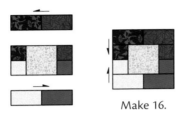

Make 16.

Assembling the Quilt Top

1. Lay out your blocks in four rows of four blocks each, referring to the photo on page 24 as needed. Sew the blocks together in rows. Press the seam allowances in the opposite direction from row to row.
2. Sew the rows together and press the seam allowances in one direction.

Adding Borders

1. For the side inner borders, sew the purple 32½"-long strips to the sides of your quilt center. Press the seam allowances toward the inner border.
2. To make the left outer border sew together four blue and four yellow 4½" squares. To make the right outer border sew together four red and four green squares. Press the seam allowances in one direction. Stitch these to the sides of your quilt top. Press the seam allowances toward the purple inner border.

Left border

Right border

3. Sew the three purple 1½" x 42" inner-border strips together end to end. From this strip, cut two 42½"-long strips. Stitch these strips to the top and bottom of your quilt top. Press the seam allowances toward the inner border.
4. For the top outer border, sew one yellow square, five blue squares, four red squares, and two

purple rectangles together as shown. For the bottom outer border, sew one red square, five green squares, four yellow squares, and two purple rectangles together as shown. Press the seam allowances as indicated. Stitch the borders to your quilt top, pressing the seam allowances toward the purple inner border.

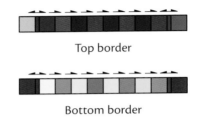

Top border

Bottom border

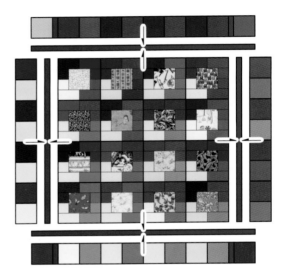

Finishing Your Quilt

1. Assemble the quilt sandwich and quilt as desired.
2. Using the purple 2¼"-wide strips, make and attach double-fold binding.

Piggy Bank Tip

Design Option

Why not use fabric printed photos as the centers of your blocks? It would make a wonderful keepsake for a family member. Another possible option is to use flannel squares to make your quilt, which is just the right size for snuggling up to watch TV.

Fortune Cookie

Designed and pieced by Claudia Plett; machine quilted by Le Ann Weaver

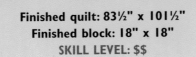

Finished quilt: 83½" x 101½"
Finished block: 18" x 18"
SKILL LEVEL: $$

For our Fortune Cookie recipe, you'll need four dimes for each cookie block. So gather up some of those beautiful Asian print dimes and get ready to quickly whip up a Fortune Cookie masterpiece!

Materials

DIMES

30 large-scale Asian print dimes for blocks

ADDITIONAL FABRIC AND SUPPLIES

2⅝ yards of white-on-white print for block
    background
2⅝ yards of black print for blocks, outer border,
    and binding
2½ yards of red print for blocks and borders
8 yards of fabric for backing
88" x 106" piece of batting

Cutting

From *each of 20* Asian print dimes, cut:
1 square, 9" x 9" (20 total)

**From *each* of the remaining Asian print
dimes, cut:**
4 squares, 5" x 5" (40 total; keep like fabrics
    together)

From the white-on-white print, cut:
5 strips, 5" x 42"; crosscut into 40 squares, 5" x 5"
20 strips, 1½" x 42"; crosscut each strip into:
    1 rectangle, 1½" x 14½" (20 total)
    2 rectangles, 1½" x 12½" (40 total)
10 strips, 1½" x 42"; crosscut into 20 rectangles,
    1½" x 14½"
9 border strips, 1½" x 42"

From the red print, cut:
5 border strips, 4½" x 42"
20 strips, 2½" x 42"; crosscut each strip into:
    1 rectangle, 2½" x 18½" (20 total)
    1 rectangle, 2½" x 16½" (20 total)
    2 squares, 2½" x 2½" (40 total)
5 border strips, 1½" x 42"

From the black print, cut:
5 border strips, 4½" x 42"
10 strips, 2½" x 42"; crosscut each strip into:
    1 rectangle, 2½" x 14½" (10 total)
    2 rectangles, 2½" x 12½" (20 total)
5 strips, 2½" x 42"; crosscut into 10 rectangles,
    2½" x 14½"
10 binding strips, 2¼" x 42"

Making the Blocks

Directions in steps 1–3 are for making one pair of blocks. Repeat to make a total of 20 blocks. After sewing each seam, press the seam allowances in the direction indicated by the arrows

1. Sew four matching 5" Asian print squares and four white squares together as shown to make two four-patch units.

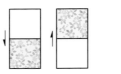

2. Cut both four-patch units into quarters diagonally as shown to make two sets of triangles, keeping like triangles together in a set. You'll have four triangle units with the print on the right side, and four triangles with the print on the left side.

Make 4 of each.

Fortune Cookie

3. Using one set of matching triangle units, sew triangles to opposite sides of a 9" Asian print square. Then sew triangles to the two remaining sides of the square. Your finished blocks should measure a scant 12½" square. In the same manner, sew matching triangle units to a second 9" Asian print square. Notice that the two blocks are a mirror image of each other. This gives the illusion that your blocks are spinning in either a clockwise or a counterclockwise direction.

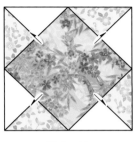 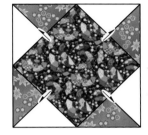

Make 10.   Make 10.

4. To frame the blocks, sew 1½" x 12½" white rectangles to opposite sides of each block. Press the seam allowances toward the white rectangles. Then sew 1½" x 14½" white rectangles to the top and bottom of each block. Your blocks should measure 14½" square. Make 20.

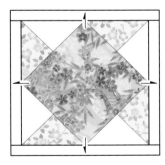

5. Sew a red square to one end of each 12½"-long black rectangle. Sew a red square to one end of each 14½"-long black rectangle. Make 20 of each.

Make 20 of each.

6. Sew the shorter units to the right side of each block, and then sew the longer units to the bottom of each block as shown, making sure you have a red square at the upper right and lower left of your block. Press the seam allowances toward the black rectangles.

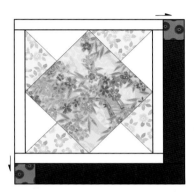

7. Sew a 16½"-long red rectangle to the left side of each block. Then sew an 18½"-long red rectangle to the top of each block. Press the seam allowances toward the red rectangle. Your blocks should measure 18½" x 18½". Make 20 blocks.

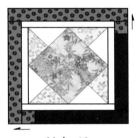 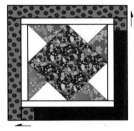

Make 10.   Make 10.

Assembling the Quilt Top

On our quilt, we positioned the blocks according to the direction they spin. The blocks that spin in a clockwise direction are on the right side of the quilt, and the blocks that spin in a counterclockwise direction are on the left side.

1. On your design wall, arrange the blocks in five rows of four blocks each. When you have an arrangement that pleases you, stitch the blocks together in rows. Press the seam allowances in the opposite direction from row to row.

2. Sew the rows together and press the seam allowances in one direction. The quilt center should measure 72½" x 90½".

Adding Borders

1. For the first inner border, stitch the 1½"-wide red border strips together end to end. Cut one 90½"-long strip and sew it to the right side of your quilt center. Cut one 73½"-long strip and sew it to the bottom of your quilt center. Press the seam allowances toward the red borders.

2. For the second inner border, stitch the 1½"-wide white border strips together end to end. From the long strip, cut two 91½"-long strips and sew them to opposite sides of your quilt top. Cut two 75½"-long strips and sew them to the top and bottom of your quilt top. Press the seam allowances toward the quilt center.

3. Sew the 4½"-wide red border strips together end to end. Sew the 4½"-wide black strips together end to end. Stitch the borders to the quilt top, mitering the corners and referring to "Borders with Mitered Corners" (page 73). We found it visually pleasing to position the black strips along the right side and bottom of the quilt top,

and the red strips on the left side and top of the quilt top.

Finishing Your Quilt

1. Assemble the quilt sandwich and quilt as desired.
2. Using the 2¼"-wide black binding strips, make and attach double-fold binding.

Piggy Bank Tip

Two for One

Why not make two quilts from 24 blocks—one with blocks that spin one way and one with blocks that spin the other? Framing the blocks could be optional for two really quick and easy quilts.

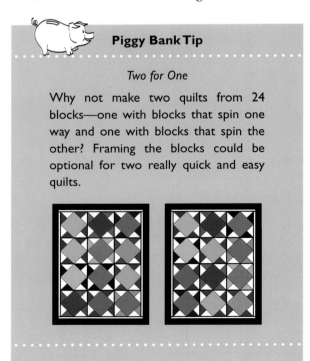

Fort Knox

Designed, pieced, and machine quilted by Le Ann Weaver

Finished quilt: 60½" x 60½"
Finished block: 12" x 12"
SKILL LEVEL: $

This Americana quilt is a great project to make for friends or family members that are in the military, or for Quilts of Valor. This quilt is sure to instill a feeling of honor and patriotism.

Quilts of Valor

A Quilt of Valor is a quilt made to honor soldiers who are wounded in war. For more information, go to www.qovf.org.

Materials

FABRIC	YOUR CHOICE OF:		
	NICKELS	DIMES	FAT QUARTERS
Assorted red prints for blocks and border	98	25	8
Assorted blue prints for blocks and border	67	17	5
Assorted gold prints for blocks and border	41	11	4
Assorted cream prints for blocks and border	19	5	2

Additional Fabric and Supplies

4 yards of fabric for backing
⅝ yard of blue print for binding
65" x 65" piece of batting

Cutting

Fabric	Your choice of:		
	Nickels	**Dimes**	**Fat Quarters**
Assorted Red prints	**From** *each of 8* **nickels, cut:** 2 rectangles, 2½" x 5" (16 total) **From** *each of 64* **nickels, cut:** 2 rectangles, 2½" x 4½" (128 total) **From** *each of 26* **nickels, cut:** 4 squares, 2½" x 2½" (104 total)	**From** *each of 8* **dimes, cut:** 2 rectangles, 2½" x 5" (16 total) 2 rectangles, 2½" x 4½" (16 total) 8 squares, 2½" x 2½" (64 total) **From** *each of 5* **dimes, cut:** 4 rectangles, 2½" x 4½" (20 total) 8 squares, 2½" x 2½" (40 total) **From** *each of 12* **dimes, cut:** 8 rectangles, 2½" x 4½" (96 total; 4 are extra)	**From** *each* **of the 8 fat quarters, cut:** 2 rectangles, 2½" x 5" (16 total) 16 rectangles, 2½" x 4½" (128 total) 13 squares, 2½" x 2½" (104 total)
Assorted blue prints	**From** *each of 16* **nickels, cut:** 2 rectangles, 2½" x 5" (32 total) **From** *each of 35* **nickels*, cut:** 4 squares, 2½" x 2½" (140 total) **Set aside the remaining 16 nickels for the blocks.*	**From** *each of 16* **dimes, cut:** 1 square, 5" x 5" (16 total) 2 rectangles, 2½" x 5" (32 total) 8 squares, 2½" x 2½" (128 total) **From 1 dime, cut:** 12 squares, 2½" x 2½"	**From** *each of 4* **fat quarters, cut:** 4 squares, 5" x 5" (16 total) 8 rectangles, 2½" x 5" (32 total) 24 squares, 2½" x 2½" (96 total) **From 1 fat quarter, cut:** 44 squares, 2½" x 2½"
Assorted gold prints	**From** *each of 8* **nickels, cut:** 2 rectangles, 2½" x 5" (16 total) **From** *each of 33* **nickels, cut:** 4 squares, 2½" x 2½" (132 total)	**From** *each of 8* **dimes, cut:** 2 rectangles, 2½" x 5" (16 total) 12 squares, 2½" x 2½" (96 total) **From** *each of 2* **dimes, cut:** 16 squares, 2½" x 2½" (32 total) **From 1 dime, cut:** 4 squares, 2½" x 2½"	**From** *each of 3* **fat quarters, cut:** 6 rectangles, 2½" x 5" (18 total; 2 are extra) 30 squares, 2½" x 2½" (90 total; 2 are extra) **From 1 fat quarter, cut:** 44 squares, 2½" x 2½"
Assorted cream prints	**From** *each of 3* **nickels*, cut:** 4 squares, 2½" x 2½" (12 total) **Set aside the remaining 16 nickels for the blocks.*	**From** *each of 4* **dimes, cut:** 4 squares, 5" x 5" (16 total) **From 1 dime, cut:** 12 squares, 2½" x 2½"	**From** *each of 2* **fat quarters, cut:** 8 squares, 5" x 5" (16 total) 6 squares, 2½" x 2½" (12 total)
Blue print for binding	7 strips, 2¼" x 42"		

Making the Blocks

1. Sew 16 blue and 16 red 2½" x 5" rectangles together in pairs as shown. Press the seam allowances toward the blue rectangle. Cut each pair into two 2½" x 4½" units as shown. In the same manner, sew 16 gold rectangles and the remaining blue rectangles together in pairs, press, and cut as before.

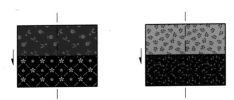

2. Sew one blue/red unit and one gold/blue unit together to make a four-patch unit as shown. Press the seam allowances to one side. Make 32 four-patch units.

Make 32.

3. Sew one red 2½" x 4½" rectangle and one four-patch unit together, making sure to position the four-patch unit as shown. Sew a blue 2½" square to one end of a red 2½" x 4½" rectangle and press the seam allowances toward the rectangle. Sew the units together as shown to make one A unit; press. Your unit should measure 6½" x 6½". Make 32 A units.

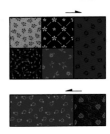 

Unit A.
Make 32.

4. Referring to "Creating Half-Square-Triangle Units" (page 71), draw a diagonal line on the wrong side of the cream 5" squares. Make 32 half-square-triangle units using the cream squares and the blue 5" squares. Press the seam allowances toward the blue triangles.

Make 32.

5. Sew a red 2½" x 4½" rectangle to each half-square-triangle unit as shown. Press the seam allowances toward the rectangle. Sew a red 2½" square to one end of a red 2½" x 4½" rectangle; press. Then sew the units together as shown to make a B unit and press. Your unit should measure 6½" x 6½". Make 32 B units.

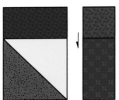 

Unit B.
Make 32.

6. Lay out two A units and two B units, rotating the units as shown. Sew the units together to complete the block. Your block should measure 12½" x 12½". Make 16 blocks.

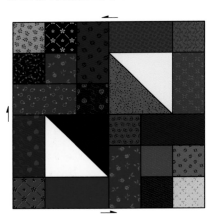

Make 16.

Assembling the Quilt Top

1. Rotate and join your blocks as shown to make four rows of four blocks each. Press the seam allowances in the same direction in each row.

Make 4.

2. Sew the rows together, rotating every other row to form diagonal pathways across your quilt top and press. Your quilt top should measure 48½" x 48½".

Adding the Borders

1. Using 2½" squares, sew together three blue squares, two red squares, and four gold squares in the color placement as shown. We suggest pressing the seam allowances open. Your blocks should measure 6½" x 6½". Make 32 border blocks.

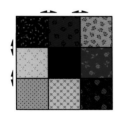

Border block.
Make 32.

2. For the corner blocks, sew together three blue squares, two red squares, one gold square, and three cream squares as shown; press the seam allowances open. Your blocks should measure 6½" x 6½". Make 4 corner blocks.

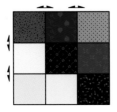

Corner block.
Make 4.

3. Create two side borders of eight border blocks each, rotating the blocks as shown. Create two borders of eight border blocks each for the top and bottom borders, rotating the blocks, and then sew a corner block on each end of the borders as shown. Press the seam allowances as indicated.

Side border.
Make 2.

Top/bottom border.
Make 2.

4. Sew the borders to the sides, and then the top and bottom of your quilt top. Press the seam allowances toward the outer border.

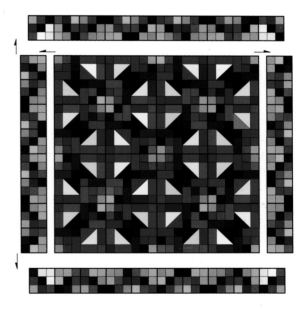

Finishing Your Quilt

1. Assemble the quilt sandwich and quilt as desired.
2. Using the blue 2¼"-wide binding strips, make and attach double-fold binding.

Golden Goose

Designed and pieced by Claudia Plett; machine quilted by Le Ann Weaver

Finished quilt: 72½" x 88½"
Finished block: 8" x 8"
SKILL LEVEL: $$

For a versatile quilt design, try our Golden Goose! It's a lot quicker than it looks, with quick flying-geese units. Imagine this quilt in a rich assortment of scrappy plaids, cozy flannels, red and green for the holidays, or in black-and-white prints—we could go on and on!

Materials

NICKELS

168 assorted yellow background prints for blocks (or 42 dimes)

DIMES

42 assorted gold prints for blocks

ADDITIONAL FABRIC AND SUPPLIES

1⅝ yards of gold fabric for inner border and binding
5⅝ yards of fabric for backing
77" x 92" piece of batting

Cutting

From *each* of the yellow background nickels, cut:
1 square, 4⅞" x 4⅞" (168 total)

From *each* of the gold dimes, cut:
1 square, 9¼" x 9¼" (42 total)

From the gold fabric, cut:
7 strips, 4½" x 42"
9 strips, 2¼" x 42"

Making the Blocks

1. With a light-colored pencil, mark a diagonal line on the wrong side of each yellow background square. Mix up your squares.

2. To create flying-geese units for your blocks, place two yellow squares on opposite corners of a gold square, right sides together. The yellow squares will overlap a little and the diagonal line should extend across the squares from corner to corner; pin in place if needed. Stitch a scant ¼" seam allowance on both sides of the drawn line. Cut the square apart on the marked line to yield two units. Press the seam allowances toward the yellow print.

3. With right sides together, place a yellow square on the corner of one unit as shown. The drawn line should extend from the point of the corner to the point between the two yellow squares. Sew a scant ¼" seam allowance on both sides of the drawn line. Cut the unit apart on the marked line and press the seam allowances toward the yellow triangles. In the same manner sew a yellow square on the second unit. You will have four flying-geese units.

Make 4 flying-geese units.

4. Repeat steps 2 and 3 using the remaining 41 gold squares and marked yellow squares. Make a total of 168 flying-geese units.

5. Sew the flying-geese units together in pairs as shown. Press the seam allowances as indicated. Your blocks should measure 8½" x 8½". Make 68 A blocks and 16 B blocks.

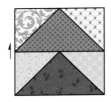
Block A.
Make 68.

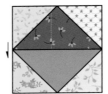
Block B.
Make 16.

Assembling the Quilt Top

1. Create rows by joining your blocks into double rows, rotating the blocks as shown. Using 12 A blocks each, make two of double-row A for the top and bottom of the quilt center. Using eight A blocks and four B blocks each, make two of double-row B for the center of the quilt top.

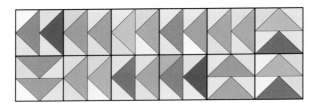
Double-row A.
Make 2.

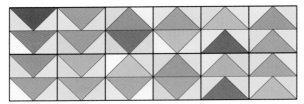
Double-row B.
Make 2.

2. Sew the rows together, rotating the bottom double-row A as shown to complete the quilt center. The flying-geese units should be circling the quilt center.

Adding Borders

1. For the inner border, sew the 4½"-wide gold strips together end to end. Referring to "Adding Borders" (page 73), measure the length of the quilt center; it should measure 64½" long. Cut two strips to this length and sew them to the sides of your quilt center. Press the seam allowances toward the inner border. Measure the width of the quilt top, including the borders; it should measure 56½". Cut two strips to this length and sew them to the top and bottom of your quilt center; press.

2. Sew eight A blocks and one B block together as shown to make a side outer border. Make two and sew them to the sides of your quilt top. Press the seam allowances toward the inner border.

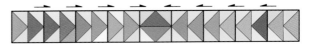
Make 2.

3. For the top and bottom borders, sew six A blocks and three B blocks together as shown. Make two and sew them to the top and bottom of your quilt. Press the seam allowances toward the inner border.

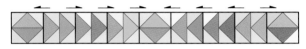

Make 2.

Finishing Your Quilt

1. Assemble the quilt sandwich and quilt as desired.
2. Using the 2¼"-wide gold strips, make and attach double-fold binding.

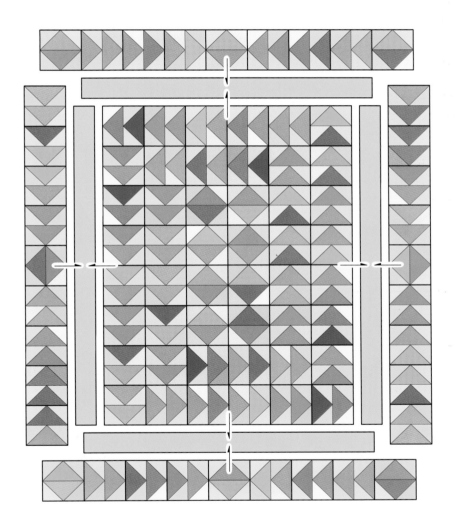

Liquid Assets

Designed and pieced by Claudia Plett; machine quilted by Le Ann Weaver

Finished quilt: 80½" x 98"
Finished block: 17½" x 17½"
SKILL LEVEL: $$

You'll find this quilt is as fun to shop and swap for as it is to make! Large-scale fish prints for the portholes combined with small-scale ocean prints in the background make it a visually fascinating quilt.

Materials

DIMES

20 assorted fish prints for blocks
80 assorted bluish green prints for blocks

ADDITIONAL FABRIC AND SUPPLIES

2⅓ yards of brown (wood-grain) print for blocks, inner border, and binding
¾ yard *each* of 2 bluish green prints for outer border
2⅜ yards of 16"-wide fusible web for machine appliqué
7½ yards of fabric for backing
84" x 102" piece of batting

Cutting

From the brown print, cut:
10 strips, 2¼" x 42"
9 strips, 1½" x 42"

From *each* bluish green print for the outer border, cut:
5 strips, 4½" x 42" (10 total)

Making the Blocks

1. With a light-colored pencil, mark a diagonal line in both directions on the wrong side of 40 bluish green dimes.
2. Place a marked dime on top of an unmarked bluish green dime, right sides together. Stitch ¼" from both sides of one of the marked lines.

Cut apart on the line, yielding two half-square-triangle units. Press the seam allowances to one side. Repeat using the remaining dimes. Make a total of 80 units.

Make 80.

3. Randomly place two units right sides together, nesting along the seam lines as shown. With a marking pencil, extend the diagonal line into the unmarked triangle. Stitch ¼" from both sides of the marked line as before. Cut apart on the marked line, yielding two quarter-square-triangle units. Press as indicated, referring to "Pressing" (page 70). Your units should measure 9¼" x 9¼". Make 80 units.

Make 80.

4. Sew together four units as shown to make one block. Your block should measure 18" x 18". Make 20 blocks.

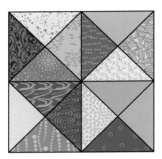

Make 20.

Adding the Appliqué

1. To create the appliquéd "portholes" in the center of the blocks, use a dark pencil or permanent marker to draw a 7"-diameter circle in the center of the fish-print dimes. (See "Piggy Bank Tip" below.) Cutting ¼" outside the drawn line, cut out each circle. Fold each circle in quarters and finger-press to create centering lines. Pin each circle in place, aligning the creases with the seam lines on the block as shown. Machine stitch on the marked line. Carefully trim away the excess fabric behind the porthole, leaving at least ¼" seam allowance. Repeat for all 20 blocks.

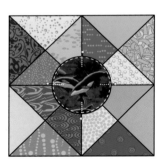

Make 20.

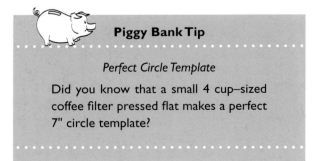

Piggy Bank Tip

Perfect Circle Template

Did you know that a small 4 cup–sized coffee filter pressed flat makes a perfect 7" circle template?

2. Referring to "Fusible Appliqué" (page 72) and using the pattern on page 43, prepare 40 half circles using fusible web and the brown print. To get the most pieces with the least amount of waste, position the template as shown.

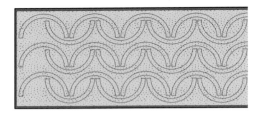

3. Fuse two half circles in place, covering the raw edges of your fish circle as shown, overlapping the ends as needed. Machine blanket stitch around the inner and outer edges of the circle using matching thread. Make 20 blocks.

Make 20.

4. Arrange the blocks in five rows of four blocks each using a design wall to obtain the arrangement you like best. Sew the blocks into rows, pressing the seam allowances in opposite directions from row to row. Sew the rows together. Your quilt top should measure 70½" x 88".

Adding the Borders

1. For the inner border, sew the 1½"-wide brown strips together end to end. Referring to "Adding Borders" (page 73), cut two strips the length of the quilt for the sides. Add the side borders, pressing the seam allowances toward the borders. Measure the width of the quilt and cut two strips for the top and bottom borders. Add the top and bottom borders and press.

2. For the outer border, sew five matching 4½"-wide bluish green strips together end to end and label as color A. Measure the length of your quilt and cut one strip to this length. Sew the

strip to the right side of your quilt top. Press the seam allowances toward the outer border.

3. Sew the remaining five matching blue green strips together end to end and label as color B. In the same manner, measure, cut, and sew a strip to the left side of your quilt top and press.

4. Measure the width of the quilt and cut one color A strip and one color B strip. Sew the A strip to the top of your quilt and the B strip to the bottom of your quilt, pressing the seam allowances toward the outer border.

Finishing Your Quilt

1. Assemble the quilt sandwich and quilt as desired.
2. Using the 2¼"-wide brown strips, make and attach double-fold binding.

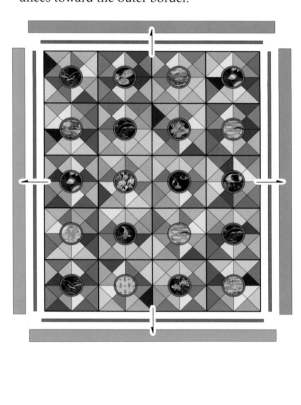

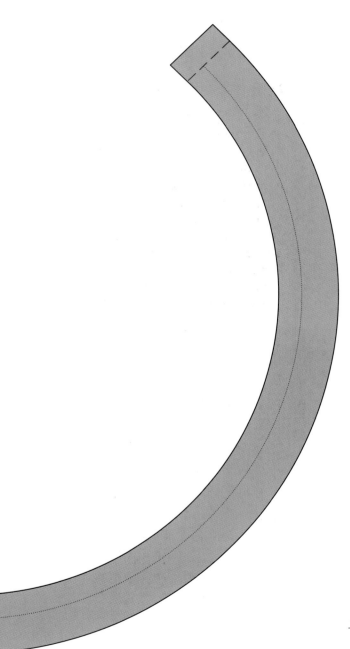

Porthole

Nickelodeon

Designed, pieced, and machine quilted by Le Ann Weaver

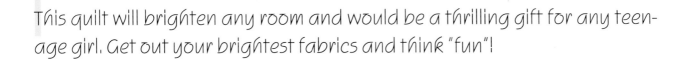

Finished quilt: 72½" x 84½"
Finished block: 12" x 12"
SKILL LEVEL: $$

This quilt will brighten any room and would be a thrilling gift for any teen-age girl. Get out your brightest fabrics and think "fun"!

Materials

FABRIC	YOUR CHOICE OF:		
	NICKELS	DIMES	FAT QUARTERS
Assorted bright prints (lime green, orange, pink, salmon, and fuchsia) for blocks and outer border	266	64	21
Assorted bright yellow prints for blocks	60	15	5

Additional Fabric and Supplies

2⅜ yards of white fabric for blocks and inner border
5¼ yards of fabric for backing
⅔ yard of lime green fabric for binding
77" x 89" piece of batting

Cutting

FABRIC	YOUR CHOICE OF:		
	NICKELS	DIMES	FAT QUARTERS
Assorted bright prints	From *each of 182* nickels, cut: 2 rectangles, 2½" x 5" (364 total) From *each of 60* nickels, cut: 4 squares, 2½" x 2½" (240 total) From *each of 24* nickels, cut: 1 square, 3" x 3" (24 total)	From *each of 46* dimes, cut: 8 rectangles, 2½" x 5" (368 total; 4 are extra) From *each of 15* dimes, cut: 16 squares, 2½" x 2½" (240 total) From *each of 3* dimes, cut: 9 squares, 3" x 3" (27 total; 3 are extra)	From *each of 10* fat quarters, cut: 24 rectangles, 2½" x 5" (240 total) From *each of 6* fat quarters, cut: 21 rectangles, 2½" x 5" (126 total; 2 are extra)* 4 squares, 3" x 3" (24 total)* From *each of 5* fat quarters, cut: 48 squares, 2½" x 2½" (240 total) *Refer to the cutting diagram on page 46.
Assorted bright yellow prints	From *each of 60* nickels, cut: 2 rectangles, 2½" x 4½" (120 total)	From *each of 15* dimes, cut: 8 rectangles, 2½" x 4½" (120 total)	From *each of 5* fat quarters, cut: 24 rectangles, 2½" x 4½" (120 total)

Additional Cutting

From the white fabric, cut:
2 strips, 3" x 42"; crosscut into 24 squares, 3" x 3"
20 strips, 2½" x 42"; crosscut into 120 rectangles, 2½" x 6½"
7 border strips, 2½" x 42"

From the lime green fabric, cut:
9 strips, 2¼" x 42"

2½" x 5"	2½" x 5"	2½" x 5"
2½" x 5"	2½" x 5"	2½" x 5"
2½" x 5"	2½" x 5"	2½" x 5"
2½" x 5"	2½" x 5"	2½" x 5"
2½" x 5"	2½" x 5"	2½" x 5"
2½" x 5"	2½" x 5"	3" x 3" / 3" x 3"
2½" x 5"	2½" x 5"	3" x 3" / 3" x 3"

Cutting diagram

Making the Blocks

1. Randomly sew the assorted bright 2½" x 5" rectangles together lengthwise in pairs. Make 182 rectangle pairs. Cut the rectangle pairs into two 2½" x 4½" units as shown.

2. Randomly mix and match the units from step 1 to make four-patch units as shown. Press as indicated, referring to "Pressing" (page 70). Make 120 units for blocks and 62 units for the outer border (set these aside).

Make 182.

3. Refer to "Creating Quick Corner Units" (page 71). Draw a diagonal line on the wrong side of each assorted bright 2½" square. Place a square on one end of a bright yellow rectangle, making sure to position the square exactly as shown. Sew on the diagonal line, trim, flip, and press. Make 120.

Make 120.

4. In the same manner, use assorted bright 2½" squares and the white rectangles to make 120 white units, making sure to position the squares exactly as shown.

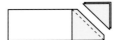 

Make 120.

5. Lay out a bright yellow unit from step 3 and a four-patch unit exactly as shown. Sew the units together and press the seam allowances toward the yellow unit. Then add a white unit to the adjacent side exactly as shown to make a quarter-block unit. Press the seam allowances toward the white unit. Your unit should measure 6½" x 6½". Make 120.

Make 120.

6. Sew together four quarter-block units, rotating them as shown. Press as indicated, referring to "Pressing." Your block should measure 12½" x 12½". Make 30 blocks.

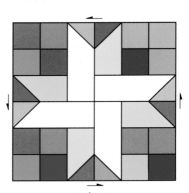

Make 30.

Assembling the Quilt

Stitch the blocks into six rows of five blocks each. Press the seam allowances in the opposite direction from row to row. Then stitch the rows together and press.

Adding the Borders

1. For the inner border, sew the white 2½"-wide strips together end to end. Referring to "Adding Borders" (page 73), measure the length of the quilt; it should measure 72½" long. Cut two strips to this length and sew them to the sides of your quilt center. Press the seam allowances toward the borders. Measure the width of the quilt, including the borders; it should measure 64½". Cut two strips to this length and sew them to the top and bottom of your quilt center and press. Your quilt center should measure 64½" x 76½".

2. For the pieced outer border, make a diagonal line on the wrong side of each white 3" square. Refer to "Creating Half-Square-Triangle Units" (page 71). Combine the marked squares and the assorted bright 3" squares to make 48 half-square-triangle units. Press the seam allowances toward the bright triangles. Trim the units to measure 2½" x 2½".

2½"

Make 48.

3. Randomly sew four half-square-triangle units together, rotating them as shown. Your diamond units should measure 4½" x 4½". Make 12 units.

Make 12.

4. Sew 17 four-patch units together to make a border unit. Join one diamond unit to each end of the border unit, rotating them as shown, to make a side border. Make two and sew them to the sides of your quilt. Press the seam allowances toward the inner border.

Side border.
Make 2.

5. Sew 14 four-patch units together to make a border unit. Join two diamond units to each end of the border unit, rotating them as shown, to make the top border. Repeat to make the bottom border. Sew the borders to the top and bottom of your quilt as shown. Press the seam allowances toward the inner border.

Top/bottom border.
Make 2.

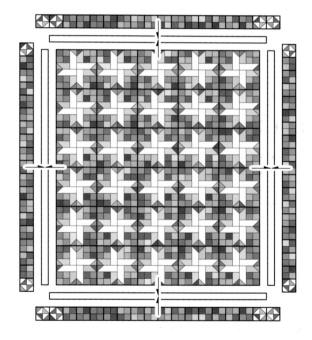

Finishing Your Quilt

1. Assemble the quilt sandwich and quilt as desired.
2. Using the lime green 2¼"-wide strips, make and attach double-fold binding.

Oscar's Treasures

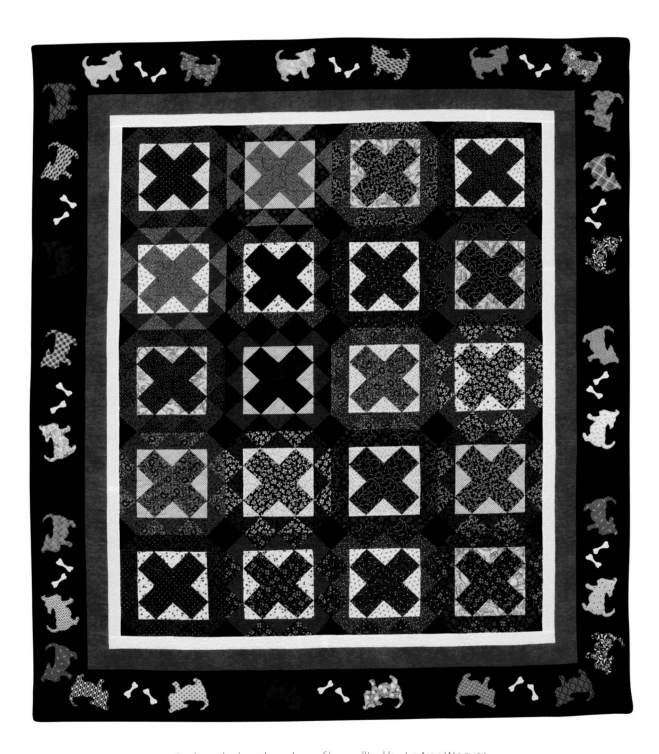

Designed, pieced, and machine quilted by Le Ann Weaver

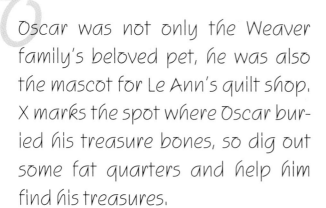

Finished quilt: 68½" x 80½"
Finished block: 12" x 12"
SKILL LEVEL: $$

Oscar was not only the Weaver family's beloved pet, he was also the mascot for Le Ann's quilt shop. X marks the spot where Oscar buried his treasure bones, so dig out some fat quarters and help him find his treasures.

. . . .

Materials

FAT QUARTERS

10 assorted small-scale black prints for blocks
10 assorted small-scale red prints for blocks
5 assorted small-scale white prints for blocks

NICKELS

28 assorted black/white and red/black prints for
    appliqué or use scraps from blocks (optional)
3 assorted white prints for appliqué (optional)

ADDITIONAL YARDAGE

2½ yards of black solid fabric for blocks, outer
    border, and binding
½ yard of white fabric for inner border
⅔ yard of red fabric for middle border
1¾ yards of 16"-wide fusible web for machine
    appliqué (optional)
5¼ yards of fabric for backing
73" x 85" piece of batting

Cutting

When cutting squares for the blocks, keep like fabrics together.

From the black solid fabric, cut:
7 strips, 6½" x 42"
8 strips, 2¼" x 42"
40 squares, 3" x 3"

From *each* assorted small-scale red print fat quarter, cut:
4 squares, 3" x 3" (40 total)
16 squares, 2⅞" x 2⅞" (160 total)

From *each* assorted small-scale white print fat quarter, cut:
4 squares, 5¼" x 5¼" (20 total)
8 squares, 3" x 3" (40 total)

From *each* assorted small-scale black print fat quarter, cut:
4 squares, 5¼" x 5¼" (40 total)
2 squares, 4½" x 4½" (20 total)
4 squares, 3" x 3" (40 total)
8 squares, 2⅞" x 2⅞" (80 total)

From the white fabric for inner border, cut:
6 strips, 2" x 42"

From the red fabric for middle border, cut:
7 strips, 3" x 42"

Making the Blocks

You'll be making a total of 20 blocks. Each block will consist of like fabrics, not random. To make one block you'll need:

- Assorted small-scale red prints: two 3" squares and eight 2⅞" squares

- Black solid fabric: two 3" squares

- Assorted small-scale white prints: two 3" squares and one 5¼" square

- Assorted small-scale black prints: one 4½" square, four 2⅞" squares, two 3" squares, and two 5¼" squares

1. Refer to "Creating Half-Square-Triangle Units" (page 71). Use a light-colored pencil to mark a diagonal line on the wrong side of the red 3" squares and white squares. Pair each red square right sides together with a black solid square and make four half-square-triangle units as shown. Pair each white square right sides together with an assorted black 3" square and make four half-square-triangle units as shown. Press the seam allowances toward the black triangles. Trim these units to measure 2½" x 2½".

Make 4 each.

Piggy Bank Tip

At Random

Pair up and switch fabrics so that no two blocks are identical. Also keep this idea in mind when arranging the blocks into rows.

2. To create flying-geese units, mark a diagonal line on the wrong side of each red 2⅞" square. Place two red squares on opposite corners of an assorted black 5¼" square, right sides together. The red squares will overlap a little and the diagonal line should extend across the squares from corner to corner; pin in place if needed. Stitch a scant ¼" seam allowance on both sides of the drawn line. Cut the square apart on the marked line to yield two units. Press the seam allowances toward the red print.

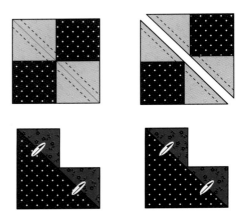

3. With right sides together, place a red square on the corner of one unit as shown. The drawn line should extend from the point of the corner to the point between the two red squares. Sew a scant ¼" seam allowance on both sides of the drawn line. Cut the unit apart on the marked line and press the seam allowances toward the red triangles. In the same manner sew a red square on the second unit. You'll have four flying-geese units, each measuring 2½" x 4½". Make four additional red/black flying-geese units (eight total).

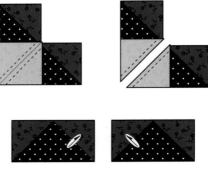

Make 8.

4. Using four assorted black 2⅞" squares and one white 5¼" square, repeat steps 2 and 3 to create four black/white flying-geese units. Press the seam allowances toward the black triangles.

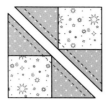 

Make 4.

5. Sew four white/black flying-geese units, four white/black half-square-triangle units, and one assorted black 4½" square together as shown to create the center of your block. Press the seam allowances as indicated. Your block center should measure 8½" x 8½".

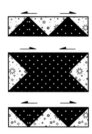 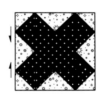

6. Join the eight black/red flying-geese units together in pairs as shown. Then sew together the flying-geese units, four black/red half-square-triangle units, and the center square from step 5 to complete your block as shown. Your block should measure 12½" x 12½". Make 20 blocks total.

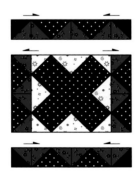 

Make 20.

Assembling the Quilt Top

1. Randomly arrange the blocks in five rows of four blocks each on your design wall to obtain the arrangement you like best. Sew the blocks into rows, pressing the seam allowances in the opposite direction from row to row.
2. Sew the rows together and press the seam allowances in one direction. Your quilt center should measure 48½" x 60½".

Adding the Borders

1. For the inner border, sew the white 2"-wide strips together end to end. Refer to "Adding Borders" on page 73 to cut two strips the length of the quilt for the sides. Add the side borders, pressing the seam allowances toward the borders. Measure the width of the quilt and cut two strips for the top and bottom borders. Add the top and bottom borders and press. Your quilt center should measure 51½" x 63½".
2. For the middle border, stitch the red 3"-wide strips together end to end. Measure, cut, and sew the borders to the sides, and then the top and bottom of the quilt top. Press the seam allowances toward the red border. Your quilt center should measure 56½" x 68½".
3. For the outer border, sew the black 6½"-wide strips together end to end. From the long strip, cut four 68½"-long strips.
4. For plain black outer borders, proceed to step 5. For the optional appliqué, use the patterns on page 52 to prepare the appliqué shapes for fusing. You will need 28 puppies (14 and 14 reversed) and 24 bones. Place three pairs of puppies and three pairs of bones on each border, and then fuse in place. The remaining four puppies are fused in place on the corners *after* the borders are attached. We recommend using a blanket stitch for securing the edges of the appliqué.

5. Attach two black outer borders to the sides of the quilt. Press the seam allowances toward the red border. Sew the remaining black outer borders to the top and bottom of the quilt and press the seam allowances toward the red border. Finish by appliquéing four puppies in the corner areas of the outer border as shown in the photo (page 48).

Finishing Your Quilt

1. Assemble the quilt sandwich and quilt as desired.
2. Using the black 2¼"-wide strips, make and attach double-fold binding.

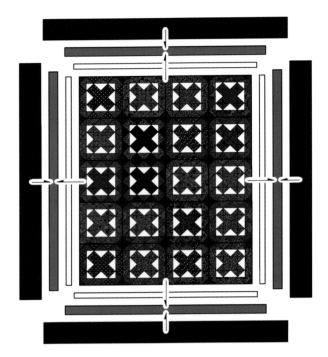

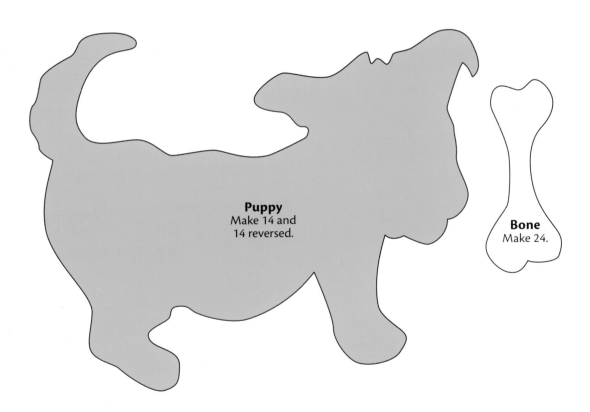

Puppy
Make 14 and
14 reversed.

Bone
Make 24.

Pumpernickel

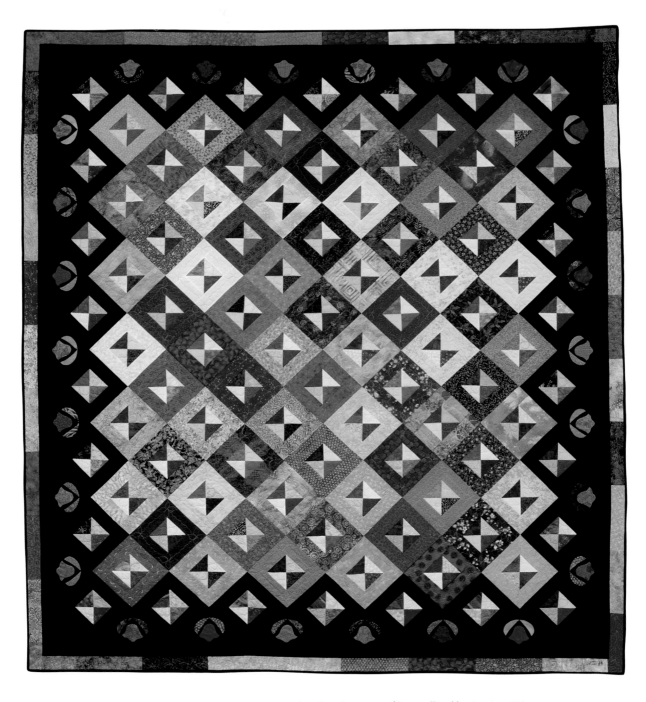

Designed, appliquéd, and pieced by Claudia Plett; machine quilted by Le Ann Weaver

Finished quilt: 85½" x 96½"
Finished block: 7¾" x 7¾"
SKILL LEVEL: $ OR $$ WITH APPLIQUÉ

For our Pumpernickel recipe, four nickels plus four dimes serves up four blocks! This very versatile design can be adapted to any color scheme or theme. If you have a collection of 2½" strips (or Jelly Rolls), you may substitute those for the dimes called for in this recipe. Appliqué is optional. A delicious way to create a quick and stunning quilt!

Materials

NICKELS

25 assorted red prints (or 7 dimes, or 3 fat quarters) for blocks

25 assorted blue prints (or 7 dimes, or 3 fat quarters) for blocks

50 assorted yellow prints (or 13 dimes, or 5 fat quarters) for blocks

13 assorted red prints (or 4 dimes, or 2 fat quarters) for appliqué (optional)

9 assorted green prints (or 3 dimes, or 1 fat quarter) for appliqué (optional)

DIMES

72 assorted prints (or 36 fat quarters) for blocks and outer border

ADDITIONAL FABRIC AND SUPPLIES

4⅛ yards of black background fabric for blocks, setting triangles, inner border, and binding

8 yards of fabric for backing

90" x 99" piece of batting

Cutting

From *each* of the dimes, cut:

4 rectangles, 2½" x 10"; crosscut 3 of the rectangles into:
- 2 rectangles, 2½" x 8¼" (144 total)*
- 2 rectangles, 2½" x 4¼" (144 total)*

Keep like rectangles together. Set aside the remaining 72 rectangles for the outer border.

From the black background fabric, cut:

9 border strips, 2½" x 42"

19 strips, 2½" x 42", crosscut into:
- 52 rectangles, 2½" x 8¼"
- 52 rectangles, 2½" x 4¼"

10 binding strips, 2¼" x 42"

7 squares, 12¼" x 12¼"; cut each square into quarters diagonally to yield 28 setting triangles (2 are extra)

2 squares, 6½" x 6½"; cut each square in half diagonally to yield 4 corner triangles

Making the Blocks

You'll be making sets of four block centers at a time. For each center set, you'll need:

- 1 red nickel
- 1 blue nickel
- 2 yellow nickels

1. Referring to "Creating Half-Square-Triangle Units" (page 71), mark a diagonal line in both directions on the wrong side of the yellow nickels. Place a yellow nickel on top of a red nickel, right sides together. Sew ¼" from both sides of one of the marked lines. Cut apart on the line and press the seam allowances toward red triangle. In the same manner, sew a yellow nickel to a blue nickel; cut apart and press the seam allowances toward the blue triangle. Make two half-square-triangle units of each color combination (four total).

Make 2 of each color combination.

2. Place a red/yellow half-square-triangle unit on top of a blue/yellow half-square-triangle unit, right sides together, so that opposite colors face each other and seams are nested as shown. With a marking pencil, extend the diagonal line into the unmarked triangle. Stitch ¼" from both sides of the marked line as before. Cut apart on the marked line, yielding two quarter-square-triangle units. Press as indicated, referring to "Pressing" (page 70). Your center units should measure 4¼" x 4¼". Make four center units for this set.

Make 4 total.

3. Repeat steps 1 and 2 to make a total of 25 sets of four center units (100 total, two are extra).
4. Sew matching 2½" x 4¼" rectangles to opposite sides of a center unit as shown. Press the seam allowances toward the rectangles. Then sew matching 2½" x 8¼" rectangles to the top and bottom of the unit to complete the block. Press the seam allowances toward the just-added rectangles. Make 72 blocks using the assorted print rectangles and 26 blocks using the black rectangles (98 blocks total).

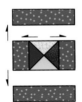

Make 72.   Make 26.

Adding the Appliqué

If you're electing not to appliqué, skip to "Assembling the Quilt Top." For our quilt, we used the hand-appliqué method described on page 72. For fusible appliqué follow the instructions in "Fusible Appliqué" (page 72).

1. Make templates for the flower and leaf shapes using the patterns on page 57. Make 26 A flowers from the 13 red print nickels (for appliqué). Make 26 B leaves and 26 C leaves from the green print nickels.
2. Using the placement guide on page 57, appliqué one A piece, one B piece, and one C piece to

each black setting triangle. Make 26 appliquéd side setting triangles.

Assembling the Quilt Top

1. Starting in the upper-right corner of your quilt, assemble one corner section as shown using one black block, one black corner triangle, and two appliquéd side setting triangles. Note the position of the triangles in the center of the block; the blue triangle is on the left, and the red triangle is on the right. Be sure to rotate the black blocks so that the block is positioned correctly at the *beginning and end* of each row. Press the seam allowances toward the setting triangles.

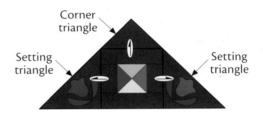

Corner triangle
Setting triangle   Setting triangle

2. Following the quilt diagram, arrange the blocks in diagonal rows. Be sure to rotate your blocks so that red triangles face red triangles and blue triangles face blue triangles. Yellow triangles are always on top and bottom. This creates a secondary optical effect for your quilt. Sew the blocks into rows, pressing the seam allowances in the opposite direction from row to row. Sew the rows together and press.

Adding Borders

1. For the inner border, sew the black 2½"-wide border strips together end to end. Refer to "Adding Borders" (page 73) to cut two strips the length of the quilt for the sides. Add the side borders, pressing the seam allowances toward the borders. Measure the width of the quilt and cut two strips for the top and bottom borders. Add the top and bottom borders and press.

2. For the outer border, sew the remaining assorted print 2½" x 10" rectangles together end to end. Press the seam allowances open to reduce bulk. Measure the length of your quilt top and cut one strip to this length. Sew the strip to the right side of the quilt top. Measure the width of the quilt top (including the just-added border) and cut one strip to that length. Sew the strip to the bottom of the quilt top. In the same manner, measure, cut, and sew the left side border, and then the top border to the quilt top. Press the seam allowances toward the newly-added borders.

Finishing Your Quilt

1. Assemble the quilt sandwich and quilt as desired.
2. Using the black 2¼"-wide binding strips, make and attach double-fold binding.

Piggy Bank Tip

Design Option

For a quicker, easier set, try using two-color centers. For example, black-and-white centers would work well as long as you don't use black or white as the block frames or the background.

"Baby Pumpernickel" is a smaller version using soft colors and a white background, with prairie points instead of binding. This quilt was designed by Claudia Plett and pieced and machine quilted by Le Ann Weaver

Leaf B
Make 26.

Flower A
Make 26.

Leaf C
Make 26.

**Appliqué patterns
and placement guide**

Twirling Dimes

Designed and pieced by Claudia Plett; machine quilted by Le Ann Weaver

Finished quilt: 92½" x 108½"
Finished block: 16" x 16"
SKILL LEVEL: $$

A rainbow of color! Each block requires five dimes—one dark, two medium, and two light. Add or subtract blocks to make your quilt larger or smaller. This quilt is great for block swaps with your friends!

Materials

DIMES

150 assorted prints in the following colors and quantities for blocks:

- Gold/yellow: 5 dark, 10 medium, 10 light
- Blue: 6 dark, 12 medium, 12 light
- Red: 7 dark, 14 medium, 14 light pink
- Purple: 4 dark, 8 medium, 8 light
- Aqua: 3 dark, 6 medium, 6 light
- Green: 2 dark, 4 medium, 4 light
- Violet: 2 dark, 4 medium, 4 light
- Brown: 1 dark, 2 medium, 2 light

23 assorted prints for outer border

ADDITIONAL FABRIC AND SUPPLIES

1¾ yards of dark blue print for inner border, outer-border corners, and binding
8¾ yards of fabric for backing
97" x 113" piece of batting

Piggy Bank Tip

Uniform Background

For a different look, you can use 3¾ yards of one background print instead of the 60 light-value dimes.

Cutting

When cutting squares and triangles for the blocks, keep like fabrics together.

From *each* of the dark dimes, cut:
1 square, 9¼" x 9¼"; cut each square into quarters diagonally to yield 4 A triangles (120 total)

From *each* of 5 medium yellow, 6 medium blue, 7 medium red, 4 medium purple, 3 medium aqua, 2 medium green, 2 medium violet, and 1 medium brown dimes, cut:
2 squares, 4⅞" x 4⅞"; cut each square in half diagonally to make 4 B triangles (120 total)
2 squares, 3" x 3" (60 total; label as F)

From the remaining medium dimes, cut:
2 squares, 4⅞" x 4⅞"; cut each square in half diagonally to make 4 C triangles (120 total)
2 squares, 3" x 3" (60 total; label as G)

From *each* of 5 light yellow, 6 light blue, 7 light pink, 4 light purple, 3 light aqua, 2 light green, 2 light violet, and 1 light brown dimes, cut:
4 squares, 4⅞" x 4⅞"; cut each square in half diagonally to yield 8 D triangles (240 total)

From the remaining light dimes, cut:
4 squares, 4½" x 4½" (120 total; label as E)

From *each* of the 23 dimes for outer border, cut:
4 squares, 4½" x 4½" (92 total)

From the dark blue print, cut:
10 border strips, 2½" x 42"
11 binding strips, 2¼" x 42"
4 squares, 4½" x 4½"

Making the Blocks

You'll be making a total of 30 blocks in eight different colors—five gold, six blue, seven red, four purple, three aqua, two green, two violet, and one brown. Each block requires a set of four A triangles, four B triangles, four C triangles, eight D triangles, four E squares, two F squares and two G squares, all from the same color family. Instructions are for making one block.

1. Sew one B triangle and one D triangle to the short sides of one A triangle as shown to make a flying-geese unit. Press the seam allowances as indicated. Sew one D triangle and one C triangle to the short sides of one A triangle as shown to make a flying-geese unit. Be sure to position the triangles exactly as shown. Your unit should measure 4½" x 8½". Make two of each.

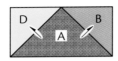
Make 2.

Make 2.

2. Sew a B triangle to a D triangle to make a half-square-triangle unit. Sew a C triangle to a D triangle to make a half-square-triangle unit. Press the seam allowances toward the dark triangle. Make two of each.

Make 2.

Make 2.

3. Refer to "Creating Quick Corner Units" (page 71). With a light-colored pencil, mark a diagonal line on the wrong side of the F and G squares. Using the E squares and the marked squares, make corner units as shown. Press the seam allowances as indicated. Make two of each.

Make 2.

Make 2.

4. Sew one unit from step 2 to one unit from step 3 as shown, making sure to follow the color placement. Your unit should measure 4½" x 8½". Press the seam allowances as indicated. Make two of each.

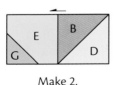
Make 2.

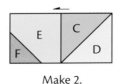
Make 2.

5. Sew a unit from step 4 to a flying-geese unit as shown to create a quadrant, making sure to follow the color placement. Press the seam allowances toward the flying-geese unit. Your quadrant should measure 8½" x 8½". Make two of each quadrant.

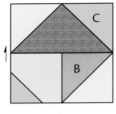
Make 2.

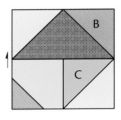
Make 2.

6. Sew the quadrants together, rotating them as shown to complete the block. Your block should measure 16½" x 16½". Press as indicated, referring to "Pressing" (page 70). Make a total of 30 blocks.

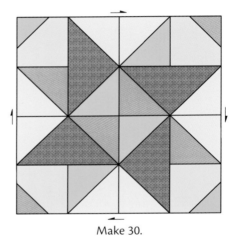
Make 30.

Assembling the Quilt Top

1. Use a design wall to arrange your blocks in six rows of five blocks each, referring to the photo (page 58) for color placement guidance. Sew the blocks into rows, pressing the seam allowances in the opposite direction from row to row.
2. Sew the rows together. Press the seam allowances in one direction. Your quilt center should measure 80½" x 96½".

Adding the Borders

1. For the inner border, sew the dark blue 2½"-wide strips together end to end. Refer to "Adding Borders" on page 73 to cut two strips the length of the quilt for the sides. Add the side borders, pressing the seam allowances toward the borders. Measure the width of the quilt and cut two strips for the top and bottom borders. Add the top and bottom borders and press. Your quilt center should measure 84½" x 100½".

2. For the side outer border, sew 25 assorted print 4½" squares together to make a border strip. Press the seam allowances open to reduce bulk. Make two and sew them to the sides of your quilt center. Press the seam allowances toward the inner border.

3. For the top and bottom outer borders, sew 21 assorted print 4½" squares together to make a border strip. Press the seam allowances open. Sew a dark blue 4½" square to each end of the strip. Make two and sew them to the top and bottom of your quilt. Press the seam allowances toward the inner border.

Finishing Your Quilt

1. Assemble the quilt sandwich and quilt as desired.
2. Using the dark blue 2¼"-wide binding strips, make and attach double-fold binding.

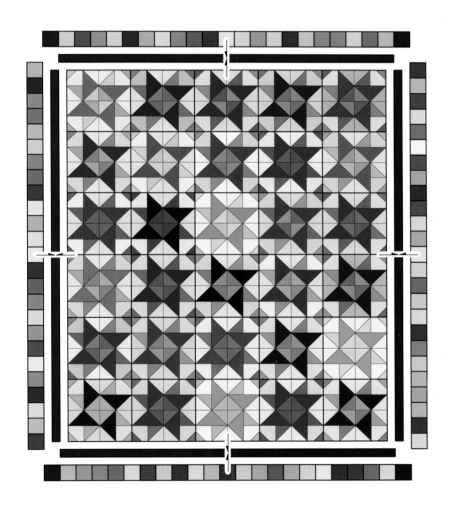

Wooden Nickel

Designed, pieced, appliquéd, and machine quilted by Le Ann Weaver

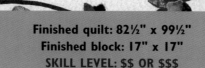

Finished quilt: 82½" x 99½"
Finished block: 17" x 17"
SKILL LEVEL: $$ OR $$$

We used lots of shortcut techniques in this quilt, making it much easier to piece than it looks! The optional appliqué makes this one a showstopper. They say, "Don't take any wooden nickels"—but we would take this one for sure!

Materials

FABRIC	YOUR CHOICE OF:	
	DIMES	FAT QUARTERS
Assorted cream background prints for blocks	6	4
Assorted cream tone-on-tone prints for blocks	38	18
Assorted aqua small-scale prints for blocks	12	4
Assorted medium red large-scale prints for blocks	15	4
Assorted medium red tone-on-tone prints for blocks	12	6
Assorted medium/dark brown large-scale prints for blocks	12	4
Assorted medium/dark brown tone-on-tone prints for blocks	12	6
Assorted medium/dark blue large-scale prints for blocks	12	4
Assorted medium/dark blue tone-on-tone prints for blocks	12	4

Additional Fabric and Supplies

15 assorted dimes *OR* 9 fat quarters of assorted prints (blues, reds, browns, and aqua) for appliqué (optional)

1⅞ yards of dark red tone-on-tone print for outer border

⅝ yard of dark blue tone-on-tone print for third border

¾ yard of dark blue fabric for binding

7¾ yards of fabric for backing

87" x 104" piece of batting

11 yards of brown ¼"-wide fusible bias tape for appliqué (optional)

2 yards of fusible web for appliqué (optional)

Appliqué pressing sheet (optional)

Cutting

Fabric	Your Choice of:	
	Dimes	**Fat Quarters**
Assorted cream background prints	**From *each of 6* dimes, cut:** 4 squares, 3½" x 3½" (24 total)	**From *each of 4* fat quarters, cut:** 6 squares, 3½" x 3½" (24 total)
Assorted cream tone-on-tone prints	**From *each of 18* dimes, cut:** 4 squares, 5" x 5" (72 total) **From *each of 20* dimes, cut:** 3 rectangles, 3" x 10" (60 total)	**From *each of 9* fat quarters, cut:** 8 squares, 5" x 5" (72 total) **From *each of 9* fat quarters, cut:** 7 rectangles, 3" x 10 (63 total; 3 are extra)
Assorted aqua small-scale prints	**From *each of 6* dimes, cut:** 4 squares, 5" x 5" (24 total) **From *each of 6* dimes, cut:** 4 squares, 3½" x 3½" (24 total)	**From *each of 4* fat quarters, cut:** 6 squares, 5" x 5" (24 total) 6 squares, 3½" x 3½" (24 total)
Assorted medium red large-scale prints	**From *each of 3* dimes, cut:** 4 squares, 4½" x 4½" (12 total) **From *each of 8* dimes, cut:** 2 rectangles, 2" x 9½" (16 total)* 2 rectangles, 2" x 6½" (16 total)* **From *each of 4* dimes, cut:** 4 rectangles, 2" x 6½" (16 total)* 4 rectangles, 2" x 3½" (16 total)*	**From *each of 4* fat quarters, cut:** 3 squares, 4½" x 4½" (12 total)* 4 rectangles, 2" x 9½" (16 total)* 8 rectangles, 2" x 6½" (32 total)* 4 rectangles, 2" x 3½" (16 total)*
Assorted medium red tone-on-tone prints	**From *each of 12* dimes, cut:** 1 square, 5¼" x 5¼" (12 total) 2 squares, 3½" x 3½" (24 total)	**From *each of 6* fat quarters, cut:** 2 squares, 5¼" x 5¼" (12 total) 4 squares, 3½" x 3½" (24 total)
Assorted medium/ dark brown large-scale prints	**From *each of 8* dimes, cut:** 2 rectangles, 2" x 9½" (16 total)* 2 rectangles, 2" x 6½" (16 total)* **From *each of 4* dimes, cut:** 4 rectangles, 2" x 6½" (16 total)* 4 rectangles, 2" x 3½" (16 total)*	**From *each of 4* fat quarters, cut:** 4 rectangles, 2" x 9½" (16 total)* 8 rectangles, 2" x 6½" (32 total)* 4 rectangles, 2" x 3½" (16 total)*

Assorted medium/ dark brown tone-on-tone prints	From *each* of the 12 dimes, cut: 1 square, 5¼" x 5¼" (12 total) 2 squares, 3½" x 3½" (24 total)	From *each* of the 6 fat quarters, cut: 2 squares, 5¼" x 5¼" (12 total) 4 squares, 3½" x 3½" (24 total)
Assorted medium/ dark blue large-scale prints	From *each* of 8 dimes, cut: 2 rectangles, 2" x 9½" (16 total)* 2 rectangles, 2" x 6½" (16 total)* From *each* of 4 dimes, cut: 4 rectangles, 2" x 6 ½" (16 total)* 4 rectangles, 2" x 3½" (16 total)*	From *each* of 4 fat quarters, cut: 4 rectangles, 2" x 9½" (16 total)* 8 rectangles, 2" x 6½" (32 total)* 4 rectangles, 2" x 3½" (16 total)*
Assorted medium/ dark blue tone-on-tone prints	From *each* of 6 dimes, cut: 4 squares, 5" x 5" (24 total) From *each* of 6 dimes, cut: 4 squares, 3½" x 3½" (24 total)	From *each* of 4 fat quarters, cut: 6 squares, 5" x 5" (24 total) 6 squares, 3½" x 3½" (24 total)

*Keep like fabrics together.

Additional Cutting

From the dark blue tone-on-tone print, cut:
8 strips, 2" x 42"

From the dark red tone-on-tone print, cut:
9 strips, 6½" x 42"

From the dark blue fabric, cut:
10 strips, 2¼" x 42"

Making the Blocks

1. Refer to "Creating Half-Square-Triangle Units" (page 71). Mark a diagonal line on the wrong side of 24 cream 5" squares. Pair each cream square with a blue 5" square and make 48 half-square-triangle units. Press the seam allowances toward the blue triangle. Trim these units to measure 4½" x 4½".

Make 48.

2. Repeat step 1 using the red 5¼" squares and the brown 5¼" squares to make 24 half-square-triangle units. Mark a diagonal line on the wrong side of the aqua 5" squares. Place aqua squares and triangle units, right sides together, with the drawn line perpendicular to the red/brown seam line as shown. (The aqua squares are slightly larger than the triangle units.) Stitch ¼" from both sides of the marked line and cut apart on the line. Press the seam allowances toward the aqua triangle. You'll have two units with mirror-image red and brown triangles. Trim the units to measure 4½" x 4½". Make 48 units total.

Make 24 each
(48 total).

3. Arrange four units from step 1, four units from step 2, and one red 4½" square, rotating the units as shown. Sew the units into rows, and then sew the rows together to make a center star

unit. Press the seam allowances as indicated. Your block should measure 12½" x 12½". Make 12 center star units.

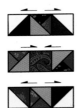

Make 12.

4. To make triangle units, sew matching red, blue, or brown 2" x 3½" rectangles to opposite sides of a cream 3½" square. Press the seam allowances toward the rectangles. Stitch matching red, blue, or brown 2" x 6½" rectangles to the top and bottom of the unit, as shown, and press. Then join matching red, blue, or brown 2" x 6½" and 2" x 9½" rectangles to the unit as shown. Press the seam allowances as indicated. Your units should measure 9½" x 9½". Make 24 units. Cut each unit in half diagonally as shown to yield 48 triangle units.

 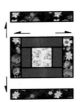

Make 24.   Make 48 triangle units.

5. Sew triangle units to opposite sides of a center star unit as shown. (See tip at upper right.) Press the seam allowances toward the triangle units. Sew triangle units to the two remaining sides of the block and press. Your block should measure 17½" x 17½". Make a total of 12 blocks.

Make 12.

Piggy Bank Tip

Make a Pinch

When joining the triangle units to the center star unit, try marking the center of each unit by folding the unit in half and pinching the fold to make a crease line. This will help you align the center of the units before stitching. You can also use this technique when you're adding setting corners on any on-point layout.

 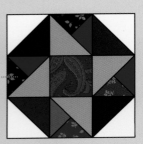

Crease, then align centers.

6. Refer to "Creating Quick Corner Units" on page 71). Draw a diagonal line on the wrong side of the remaining cream 5" squares. Place a cream square on each corner of your block as shown. Sew along the marked line, trim, and press the seam allowances toward the cream triangle. You may wish to save the discarded units to use as a border on a wall hanging or table runner (see page 68). Repeat to make a total of 12 blocks.

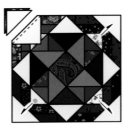 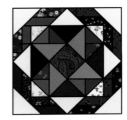

Make 12.

Assembling the Quilt Top

1. Arrange the blocks in four rows of three blocks each using a design wall to obtain the arrangement you like best. Sew the blocks together in rows, pressing the seam allowances in the opposite direction from row to row.

2. Sew the rows together and press the seam allowances in one direction. Your quilt center should measure 51½" x 68½".

Adding the Pieced Borders

1. To make the first pieced border, sew eight cream 3" x 10" rectangles together end to end and press the seam allowances open to reduce bulk. Make four strips. Sew the strips together in pairs lengthwise, staggering the seams as shown. Press the seam allowances open. Trim each border unit to measure 68½" long, and join them to the sides of your quilt top. Press the seam allowances toward the borders.

Make 2.

2. Sew seven cream 3" x 10" rectangles together end to end and press. Make four strips. In the same manner as in step 1, make two 61½"-long border units and sew them to the top and bottom of your quilt. Press. Your quilt center should measure 61½" x 78½".

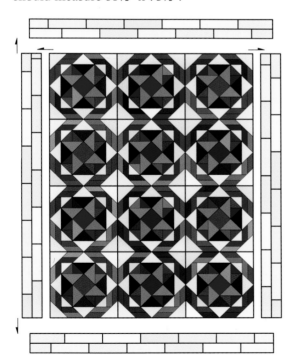

3. For the second pieced border, sew a random mix of 26 red, brown, aqua, and blue 3½" squares together to make a 78½"-long border strip. Press

the seam allowances open. Make two and sew them to the sides of your quilt top. Press the seam allowances toward the just-added borders.

4. For the top and bottom borders, sew a random mix of 22 red, brown, aqua, and blue 3½" squares together using a *scant* ¼"-wide seam allowance. Make two border strips, each measuring 67½" long. Stitch the borders to the top and bottom of your quilt top. Your quilt top should measure 67½" x 84½". (To reduce fraying while appliquéing, machine baste around your quilt top ⅛" from the outer edges.)

Adding the Appliqué

1. Using the patterns on page 69 and the 15 assorted blue, red, brown, and aqua dimes, prepare the appliqué shapes for fusing. Refer to "Fusible Appliqué" on page 72 as needed. Following the manufacturer's instructions, use an appliqué pressing sheet and the placement guides on page 69 to layer the flowers before fusing them to the cream border.

2. Apply fusible bias tape for the vines in a manner pleasing to you. Add the flowers and leaves as shown in the photo on page 62. We recommend using a machine blanket stitch for securing the edges of the appliqué.

Adding the Borders

1. For the third border, sew the dark blue 2"-wide strips together end to end. Refer to "Adding Borders" on page 73 to cut two strips the length of the quilt for the sides. Add the side borders, pressing the seam allowances toward the borders. Measure the width of the quilt and cut two strips for the top and bottom borders. Add the top and bottom borders and press. Your quilt should measure 70½" x 87½".

2. For the outer border, sew the dark red 6½"-wide strips together end to end. In the same manner as before, measure, cut, and sew the borders to the quilt top. Press the seam allowances toward the outer border.

Finishing Your Quilt

1. Assemble the quilt sandwich and quilt as desired.

2. Using the dark blue 2¼"-wide strips, make and attach double-fold binding.

"Wooden Nickel Wall Hanging" was created using only four blocks. Designed, pieced, and machine quilted by Le Ann Weaver.

The border on Le Ann's "Wooden Nickel Table Runner" is made from the leftover triangles created while sewing quick corner units for the blocks in her quilt. Designed, pieced, appliquéd, and machine quilted by Le Ann Weaver.

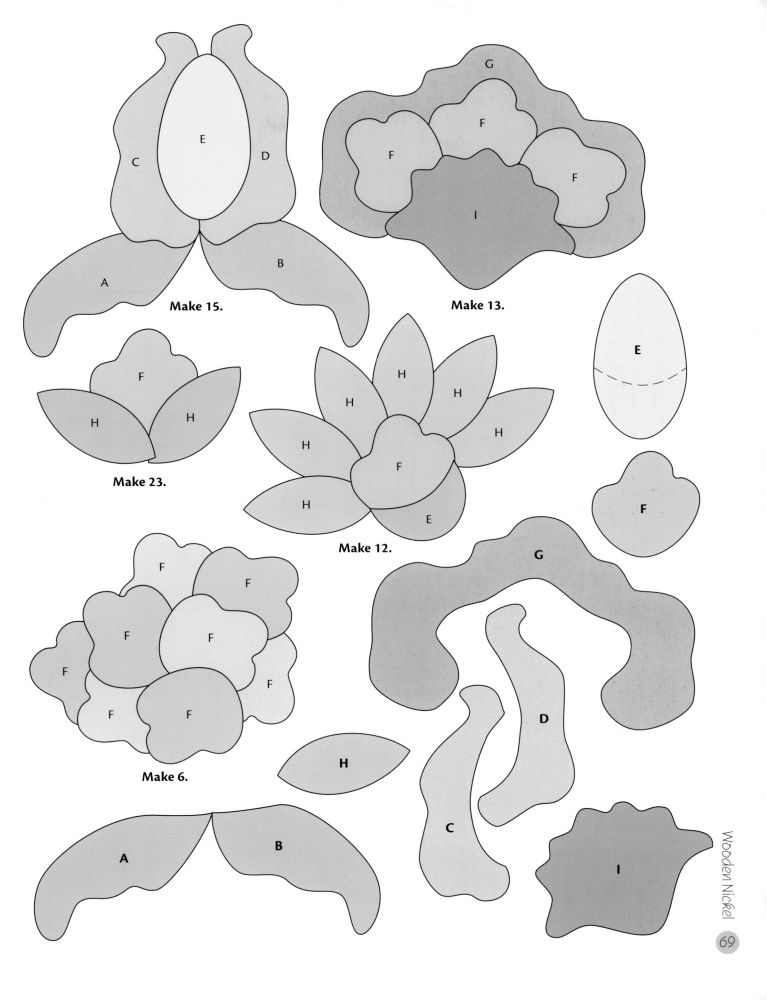

Make 15.

Make 13.

E

Make 23.

Make 12.

F

Make 6.

H

G

D

C

A

B

I

Basic Quiltmaking Instructions

In this section, we offer general instruction and helpful tips that we hope will make your quilting experience a little bit easier. Detailed quilting instructions are not included because there are many excellent books for beginning quilters available at your local quilt shop or library, covering topics such as rotary cutting and machine piecing. Many more books are available for specific quilting techniques, such as hand and machine quilting, and we encourage you to make use of these books for any additional information needed.

Tools of the Trade

In addition to the basic sewing supplies—thread, scissors, and a tape measure—these are items we feel no quilter should be without.

Rulers. We love rulers and like to buy them in all sizes, but you can easily get by with three for all the quilts in this book. We recommend a 6½" x 24", a 6½" square, and a 12½" square ruler. A 5" square ruler is helpful for cutting nickels from your stash, but this can be done with the 6½" square as well. In our quilter's heaven, there would be a square ruler in every size from 2½" to 12½"!

Walking foot. This sewing-machine attachment or built-in feature is essential for adding borders and binding and for straight-line machine quilting. Some quilters even do all of their piecing using a walking foot.

Darning foot. This foot is necessary for free-motion machine quilting.

Seam ripper. Unless you sew perfectly every time, at some point you'll need a very good seam ripper. Face it. Mistakes happen.

Flower-head pins. They're so very handy! They're easy to see, and you can write on them, which makes them good for marking row numbers and for marking arrows to indicate directions.

Cutting mats. We recommend a large one, 24" x 36". It's also handy to have a smaller one for trimming half-square-triangle units.

Large pressing surface. The bigger, the better. You can get by with a full-sized ironing board, but a wider flat surface will work better for pressing large quilt tops.

Design wall. This is a quilter's most important tool. "The bigger, the better" holds true here also. There are a number of materials you can use to make your own design wall. If you have an open wall at home, try tacking a roll of batting to it. Fabrics will temporarily adhere to the batting. Or you can use flannel mounted to a board or large piece of foam core. Another source for a design wall is a purchased flannel-backed tablecloth; spread it out on the floor or attach it to the back of a closet door.

A reliable sewing machine. Take care of your machine! Oil and service it regularly. You might do this on memorable occasions, like your birthday or anniversary, so you can remember when servicing is due. Clean out the bobbin casing after every quilt you piece. Also change the needle before starting any new project.

Pressing

We recommend an iron on the cotton setting and no steam for all pressing. Pressing with steam is only recommended when you're attempting to block the size of a piece.

Pressing and ironing are two different things. Ironing is a back-and-forth movement that can distort pieces. Pressing is strictly raising the iron up and placing the iron down on one spot.

Press after sewing each seam. "Sew and press, sew and press" is a good rule to follow. The seam allowances are almost always pressed to one side, usually toward the darker fabric. However, follow the recommended pressing directions on each project. The seam allowances are sometimes pressed open or toward the lighter fabrics to reduce bulk in certain areas or to make quilt assembly easier.

When squares are joined together with straight seams, we sometimes flip the seam allowances at the intersection of four squares to reduce bulk as shown on page 71. Do this by holding the block and using your thumb to flip or fold half of the seam allowance in one direction and the other half in the opposite direction. This will release the stitches at the center, resulting in a seam allowance that can be pressed in opposite directions. When pressed this way, the block will lie nice and flat, and you should see a tiny four-patch unit at the seam intersection.

Block Construction

Most of the quilt projects include blocks made up of smaller units. In this section we describe the techniques for making the units.

CREATING HALF-SQUARE-TRIANGLE UNITS

These units begin with squares from two fabrics, usually a light and a dark.

1. Using the two fabric squares as instructed in the project, draw a diagonal line on the wrong side of the lighter square. Place the two squares right sides together, with the marked square on top. Stitch ¼" on both sides of the marked line.

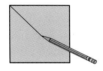

Mark on the diagonal.   Stitch ¼" on both sides of the line.

2. Cut apart on the marked line. Press the seam allowances toward the darker fabric.

Cut apart on the line.   Press toward the darker fabric.

3. Trim your units to the instructed finished measurement as follows. Your ruler should have a 45° diagonal line. Place this line along the seam line of your half-square-triangle unit, with the 1" markings at the top and the right. Set the lower left measurement to the instructed measurement on your specific project. For example, if the instructions say trim to 4½", place the lower left of your unit on the ruler's diagonal line at 4½".

Trim away the excess fabric along the top and right sides of your unit.

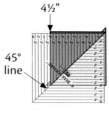

Trim excess.

CREATING QUICK CORNER UNITS

This technique is used to create a triangle on the corner of a larger unit. But instead of cutting a triangle, a square is placed on the corner, sewn on the diagonal, and then trimmed. No triangles need to be cut and no bias edges are sewn.

1. Using the square or squares as instructed in the project, mark or crease a diagonal line on the wrong side of the square. Place the square in the appropriate corner, adjusting the position of the marked line according to your project instructions. We recommend that you stitch just a hair outside that line to allow for the fabric that will be folded back.

Stitch a hair outside the marked line.

2. Trim ¼" from the stitching. Flip the triangle back and press outward. Repeat as instructed in each project.

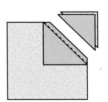

Fusible Appliqué

Fusible appliqué is a fast way to appliqué a design. All you need is fusible web, an iron, an appliqué pressing sheet for layering shapes, thread, and your sewing machine.

We recommend that you use a double-sided, lightweight fusible web. It's easy to work with and doesn't make the fabric too stiff. The appliqué pressing sheet is helpful when fusing a design of several layers, and it protects the ironing surface. Both the pressing sheet and fusible web are available at your local quilt store. Always follow the manufacturer's instructions for the fusible products you choose.

Any appliqué project in this book can be done using fusible web by reversing the pattern onto tracing paper, turning the paper over, and using the reversed image as the pattern to make your templates.

1. Trace the pattern from the book page onto the paper side of the fusible web. Cut out the pieces approximately ¼" around the design.
2. Following the manufacturer's instructions, fuse the web to the *wrong* side of the desired fabric. Let cool, and cut the shape out on the lines.
3. Peel the paper off and fuse the appliqué shape to the background using a dry iron. If you're layering shapes, follow the manufacturer's instructions for your appliqué pressing sheet.
4. To secure the outer edges of the appliqué, set your machine for a simple zigzag stitch, blanket stitch, or feather stitch. Some quilters prefer to stitch the edges by hand using a blanket stitch or whipstitch.

Keep in mind that it's much easier to appliqué individual blocks or small background sections rather than a finished top. You'll find it simpler to maneuver a small square when sewing.

Hand Appliqué

There are many ways to appliqué by hand. Our preferred method is the freezer-paper method. Freezer paper is a wax-coated paper available at most grocery stores in long rolls that are 18" wide. For information on other methods, check out appliqué books available at your local quilt store or from the library.

1. With a fine-lead pencil, mark the location for the appliqué pieces on your background fabric. Use the template patterns or placement guide, if provided, to help properly place the pieces.

2. Make a template from template plastic or cardstock using the pattern provided with the project. Or simply place the freezer paper over the pattern in the book and trace directly from the pattern page. Use the template to trace the number of pieces needed onto freezer paper. There is no need to add seam allowances.
3. Cut out the freezer-paper templates on the drawn line. Place the freezer-paper templates on the right side of the desired fabric, shiny side down, and press the paper to the fabric with a dry iron. Cut out the shapes, adding a scant ¼" seam allowance.

Freezer-paper template

¼" seam allowance

4. Turn the seam allowances under using the freezer paper as a guide and clipping inside curves when necessary. Baste the seam allowances along the edges, stitching through the freezer paper.
5. Pin your appliqué piece in position on the block. Remember to layer pieces from the bottom up—for example, a stem would be appliquéd before flower petals.

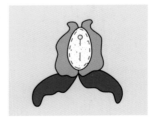

6. Stitch with a thread color that matches your appliqué piece, not the background. Make stitches approximately ⅛" apart all the way around. Be sure to stitch through all layers.

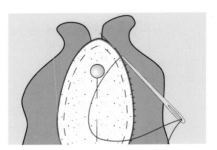

7. When stitching is complete, remove the basting stitches and gently peel away the freezer paper. Press.

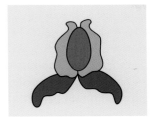

Adding Borders

Always measure your quilt through the center before cutting and adding borders. Due to slight variations in each quilter's cutting and stitching, the quilt may not be exactly the size stated in the instructions, and the edges of a quilt may stretch slightly from handling and be a bit longer than the center.

BORDERS WITH BUTTED CORNERS

1. Measure the quilt through the center vertically to determine the length to cut the side borders. Cut two border strips to this measurement, piecing if necessary.

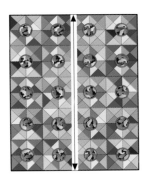

2. Fold each border strip and the quilt top in half to create a crease in the center. This will be your center reference point for pinning. Pin and sew the borders to the sides of the quilt, matching the centers and ends. Press the seam allowances toward the border strips unless the quilt project specifies otherwise.

3. Measure the quilt through the center horizontally (including the just-added borders) to determine the length to cut the top and bottom borders. Cut two border strips to this measurement, piecing if necessary.

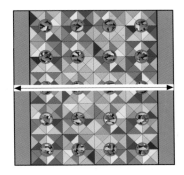

4. Sew the borders to the top and bottom of the quilt as you did the sides. Press toward the borders.

BORDERS WITH MITERED CORNERS

Sometimes a mitered border can add the perfect finishing touch to a quilt. Don't be afraid of them!

Here's a simple formula for determining how long to cut border strips for mitering. Measure the width and length of the center of the quilt.

Width (or length) + (2 x width of border) + 4"

1. Cut a border to the length determined using the formula above. Fold the border strip in half to create a crease in the center. This will be your center reference point for pinning.

2. Find the center of the side of the quilt and pin the border section to it, matching the centers.

3. Begin stitching near the center and stitch toward one end, stopping and backstitching ¼" from the edge as shown. Repeat stitching from the center to the opposite end, backstitching in the same

manner. Press the seam allowances toward the border. Repeat this step for all four sides of the quilt.

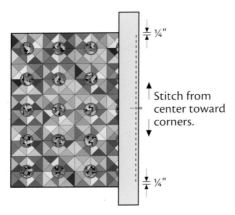

Stitch from center toward corners.

¼"

¼"

4. Trim the corners by cutting next to the raw edges as shown. Fold back one border piece along the diagonal and crease as shown. This crease will be your stitching line on the wrong side. If you wish, you can mark this diagonal line lightly with a pencil.

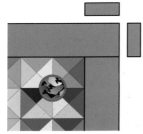

Trim corner.

Fold back and crease.

5. Working from the wrong side, bring together both border sections, right sides together, and stitch on the creased line as shown. Backstitch at the inside corner as well as the outside border edge. Trim the seam allowances to ¼" and press them open.

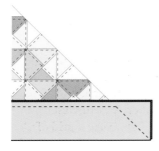

Stitch along crease line.

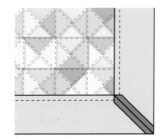

Trim and press open.

Quilting Your Quilt

Finally, it's time to quilt! Before you begin quilting, we recommend you stitch ⅛" from the outside edge of your quilt top to stabilize the grain and especially to stabilize any pieced outside borders.

There are a lot of variables when it comes to quilting. Ask yourself these questions to determine the next step to finishing your project.

Do I want to quilt this myself, or have it quilted by a professional hand or machine quilter? The answer to this question will determine whether or not the quilt should be basted, and whether it should be basted with pins for machine quilting or with thread for hand quilting. For either option, you'll need to decide on the quilting design and determine if the quilting lines need to be marked first.

How is the quilt to be used? This may determine what kind of batting or backing you intend to use, or which quilting method is to be used. You may be making a small charity quilt, and therefore, you might consider tying the layers together or machine quilting it yourself on your home machine. Or if you're making a table runner for yourself, you might want to use a very flat batting, and then quickly hand or machine quilt it yourself.

What method can I afford at this point? We all know that the expense is a factor in finishing a quilt. It may be quite expensive, for example, to have a hand quilter finish your quilt for you. If it's a wedding quilt or destined to become an heirloom, then hand quilting may be your choice. Long-arm machine quilters are another choice. Most of them can adapt your budget to the type of quilting they do on your quilt. There are some pretty amazing things going on in the long-arm quilting profession right now. You can get anything from basic stitching to extremely fancy and beautiful designs. All of the quilts in this book have been machine quilted on a long-arm machine.

There are no basting requirements when taking your quilt to a machine quilter. All you do is take your quilt top, batting, and backing (pieced together if necessary) to your long-arm quilter. You most likely will not have to do any marking on your quilt, unless by arrangement when you want a special design. Always remember to give your long-arm quilter ample backing fabric. The backing should always be at least 4" to 8" larger than your top.

Some long-arm quilters will also finish your quilt with binding, usually at an additional cost.

How much time do I have? This can be the most important question of all. If you're on a deadline, getting a long-arm machine quilter to do it for you is your best bet. However, some of them are working behind schedule, so be sure to call around first. On the other hand, if you have all the time in the world, then you can spend time doing some hand quilting. It's a most rewarding pastime.

MARKING YOUR QUILT

Choose a design that fills the space of your blocks, or leave it entirely up to your long-arm or hand quilter. Some designs require marking that will have to be done before basting the layers together. Other designs might be marked as you go. Whatever marking you do, please do a test patch to try out any pens or pencils you plan to use. Some are not suitable for some fabrics or designs. They may have too thick of a point, or perhaps the lines will disappear in humid areas, or some may set permanently when touched by an iron. Below are a few quilting design choices.

Stitching in the ditch refers to quilting along seam lines or appliquéd pieces. It requires hardly any prior markings. It's not easily done on a long-arm machine, so check with your machine quilter first if this is what you want.

Outline quilting is done an equal distance from each seam, usually ¼" away. To a seasoned quilter, no marking is required because she can "eyeball" ¼". Some quilters use ¼" masking tape to mark straight lines.

Motif quilting is usually done with hand quilting. A template or stencil is used to mark a specific design in an area to be quilted; this should be done before basting. Some long-arm quilters use light-weight paper as a pattern. The paper is removed after the stitching, and no marking is required.

Echo or shadow quilting follows the shape of an object with additional lines that run parallel to the first. This too is done by eyeballing and requires no marking.

Crosshatch quilting is a straight-line grid, often with lines 1" apart. The lines are usually marked ahead of time, but some machine quilters can do this by using a special guide.

Meandering quilting lines are curved, random, and never crossing. No marking is required.

Stippling is very closely spaced meandering. It's often used in background areas to fill the space, and no marking is required.

CHOOSING BATTING

Using the right batting will make your quilting easier. Here are some tips.

- For fine hand quilting, use a low-loft blend specifically stating that it can be used for hand quilting. Check the label for the recommended distance between quilting, such as 3", 4", 5", etc. Hand quilting with a wool or silk batting is said to be like quilting through butter. Hand quilting with some dense cotton battings can be difficult. Always test a square first.
- For quilts with dark or black backgrounds, choose a black batting if possible.
- Use high-loft batting only for tied quilts or comforters.
- Most long-arm quilters prefer a mostly cotton-blend batting, such as 80/20 cotton/polyester. Check with yours to see which type she prefers.

LAYERING AND BASTING

1. Snip any long or dark-colored threads that may show through your top. Press the quilt top carefully for a nice, smooth finish. Make sure any required marking is done before basting.
2. Remove the batting from its package and let it "breathe" for a day or two, perhaps on a bed, before using. This will relax the creases caused by tight packaging.
3. Lay your backing fabric wrong side up on a large flat surface. You may wish to use masking tape to secure the backing to the surface. It should be smooth and flat, but not stretched.
4. Place the batting on top of the backing, gently smoothing out any wrinkles.
5. Place and center the quilt top right side up on top of the batting.
6. If you're hand quilting, begin in the center of the quilt and baste with long running stitches, working your way to the outside edges. Do this in compass-point directions beginning in the center—in other words, north first, and then south, east, west, northeast, northwest, southeast, and southwest. Then baste a grid of straight lines every 6" or so.

If you're machine quilting on your home sewing machine, baste with rustproof safety pins through all layers approximately 4" apart. You can use the width of your hand as a guide for placing pins. You can remove the pins as you come to them while quilting.

If you're taking your quilt top to a long-arm quilter, no basting or layering is necessary—just be sure you provide ample backing fabric and batting. You may wish to stabilize the quilt top by stitching around the entire quilt ⅛" from the edge. This is crucial for projects with pieced borders since the seams could be pulled apart when stretched on a long-arm frame. Your long-arm quilter will thank you. Then sit back, relax, and wait for the phone call when it's ready!

Binding

Each project will say how many binding strips you'll need, whether it's for straight-grain or bias binding. Most of the time we use 2¼"-wide strips for straight-grain, double-fold bindings. However, if you make scalloped or notched edges as in "Christmas Bonus" (page 11), it's best to use 1½" single-fold, bias binding.

Consider using striped or plaid fabrics for your bindings, because they add motion to your quilt. For some quilts with a busy or strong central design, stripes or plaids may be somewhat distracting. If you have a really charming scrappy quilt, you can use your leftover scraps to piece the binding strips. Another option is to use the same color for binding that you used for the outside border. For example, on a quilt with a navy blue outside border, you may wish to use a navy blue binding to blend in. We like to use a dark binding when the outer borders are dark. Also, we like to use the same fabric for the binding that is used somewhere in the center of the quilt.

1. Square up your quilt. Check the corners with a large square ruler to make sure that they are square and lie flat. You may wish to stabilize the edges of the quilt by stitching around the entire quilt ⅛" from the edge using a walking foot.

2. Trim the batting and backing to within ¼" from the raw edge of your quilt. This will create a nicely filled binding when complete.

3. Join your binding strips end to end with a diagonal seam as shown. Trim, press the seam allowances open, fold the strip in half lengthwise with wrong sides together, and press.

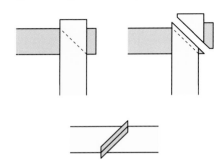

4. Use a walking foot if you have one, and begin stitching the binding to the quilt top in the middle of one side, leaving a 6" tail. Take a couple of backstitches and stitch; stop stitching ¼" from the corner as shown and backstitch. Clip the threads and remove the quilt from the machine.

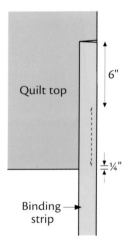

5. Turn the quilt to prepare for sewing the next side. Fold the binding away from you to create a 45° angle as shown. Then fold it back down toward you with the top fold exactly on the raw edge of your quilt. Start stitching at the top edge of your quilt and continue sewing, repeating these steps at the remaining three corners.

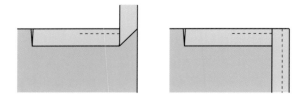

6. Stop stitching approximately 12" from the beginning; backstitch. Remove the quilt from the machine. Fold the strips back as shown and press. This creates a stitching guide for joining the ends.

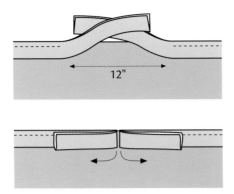

12"

7. Open the strips, match the creases and stitch on the crease line, right sides together. Trim to ¼" seam allowance. Press the seam allowances open. Finish stitching the binding to your quilt.

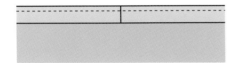

8. Working from the back of your quilt, hand stitch the binding in place with a thread color that matches the binding. Form miters at the corners as shown and stitch them closed.

Quilt back

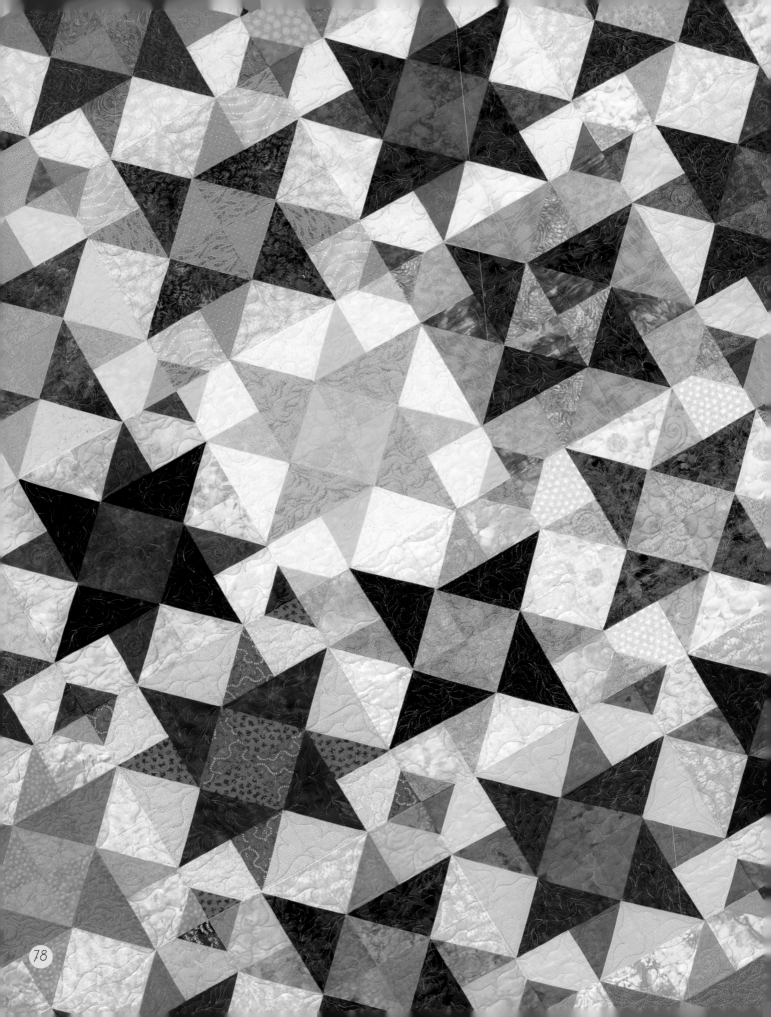

Meet the Authors

Claudia Plett and Le Ann Weaver first met in 2002, when they were both doing a mystery quilt on an Internet quilting forum. Since that time, they've become best quilting buddies! Their first book written together, *Loose Change*, was published in 2008.

They live just a few miles apart, but 45 minutes by car. Claudia resides in Inola, Oklahoma, along with her mother Elizabeth Johnson. She has three grown sons, four grand "boys," and one grand "girl." Le Ann lives in Claremore, Oklahoma, with her husband, Scott, and her son, Mitchell. She also has two grown daughters and three granddaughters.

Claudia has been quilting since before rotary cutters, and she's stopped counting the number of quilts she's made. Most of her quilts are her own original designs. Claudia's expertise in quilt design and workmanship has earned her numerous show awards and commission works. Along with being Director of the town library, she has owned a retail website since 2001, www.claudiasquiltshoppe.com. On her website, she features a monthly newsletter, photo gallery, guest gallery, free block of the month patterns, pattern page, and a humorous "Ask Granny" advice column written by her alter ego, Granny. Designing scrap and charm quilts is one of her special talents. Her hobbies in addition to quilting include reading, music, church activities, and playing with her grandchildren.

Le Ann has been a quilter for over 25 years. Along that path, she also designed and created bridal gowns and theatrical costumes. But her true passion has always been quilting. Le Ann has years of experience in designing quilts and teaching classes, as a former quilt shop owner in Tulsa. She now enjoys her online and home-based business at www.persimmonquilts.com. Le Ann also volunteers her time designing mystery quilts for the Quilts of Valor Foundation, and is codirector of a local QOV chapter. When she's not helping her husband run the family business, Le Ann enjoys going to school activities, reading, and landscaping.

There's More Online!

Discover LeAnn's mystery quilts, block-of-the-month programs,
and more at www.persimmonquilts.com.
Find more great quilt books at www.martingale-pub.com.

You might also enjoy these other fine titles from

Martingale & Company

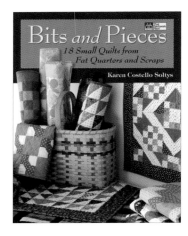

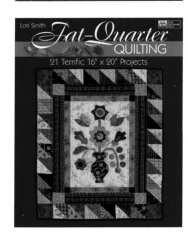

Our books are available at bookstores and your favorite craft, fabric, and yarn retailers.
Visit us at www.martingale-pub.com or contact us at:

1-800-426-3126
International: 1-425-483-3313
Fax: 1-425-486-7596
Email: info@martingale-pub.com

Martingale®
& C O M P A N Y

America's Best-Loved Craft & Hobby Books®
America's Best-Loved Knitting Books®

America's Best-Loved Quilt Books®